PACKAGE DESIGN
WORKBOOK

First published in the United States of America by
Rockport Publishers, a member of
Quayside Publishing Group
100 Cummings Center
Suite 406-L
Beverly, Massachusetts 01915-6101
Telephone: (978) 282-9590
Fax: (978) 283-2742
www.rockpub.com

Library of Congress Cataloging-in-Publication Data

DuPuis, Steven.
  Package design workbook : the art and science of successful packaging /
Steven DuPuis, and John Silva.
    p. cm.
  ISBN 1-59253-322-1
  1. Packaging--Design. 2. Commercial art. I. Silva, John. II. Braue, Kai. III.
Title.
NC1002.P33D87 2008
741.6--dc22

                                                    2008000591
                                                    CIP

10 9 8 7 6 5 4 3 2 1

ISBN-13: 978-1-59253-708-2
ISBN-10: 1-59253-708-1
Digital edition published in 2011
eISBN-13: 978-1-61673-599-9

Design: Braue-DuPuis
Cover Photography: Chris Zsarnay / Z Studios
Art Direction: Kai Braue and Marcel Robbers

Printed in China

OPEN HERE

PACKAGE DESIGN
WORKBOOK

THE ART AND SCIENCE OF SUCCESSFUL PACKAGING

BEVERLY MASSACHUSETTS

ROCKPORT PUBLISHERS

STEVEN DUPUIS
AND **JOHN SILVA**

DESIGN BY BRAUE-DUPUIS

Ingredients

Market Pantry canned pasta combines qua...
value in a rich and hearty home-style me...

Nutrition Facts

Serving Size 1 cup (252g)
Servings Per Container about 2

Amount Per Serving

Calories 270   Calories from Fat 70

	% Daily Value*
Total Fat 7g	**11%**
Saturated Fat 2.5g	**13%**
Trans Fat 0g	
Cholesterol 15mg	**5%**
Sodium 1310mg	**54%**
Total Carbohydrate 43g	**14%**
Dietary Fiber 2g	**6%**
Sugars 9g	
Protein 9g	

Vitamin A 10%	•	Vitamin C 0%
Calcium 2%	•	Iron 10%

* Percent Daily Values are based on a 2,000 calorie diet.

INGREDIENTS: WATER, TO...
TER, TOMATO PASTE), EN...
FLOUR (WHEAT FLOUR, NIACIN...
MONONITRATE, RIBOFLAVIN...
BEEF, HIGH FRUCTOSE CORN STR...
MEAL (WHEAT FLOUR, WATER...
CORN STARCH, SALT, TEXTURED...
PROTEIN (SOY FLOUR, CARAMEL C...
URAL FLAVOR, SEASONING [H...
LYZED CORN AND SOY PROTEIN, S...
LYZED CORN GLUTEN AND WHE...
ONION POWDER, CITRIC ACID...
GLUTAMATE, CARAMEL COLOR, D...
FIED CHEESE (CHEDDAR CE...
CHEESE CULTURES, SALT, ENZY...
SALT, DISODIUM PHOSPHATE), D...
RIKA, OLEORESIN CARDMON, N...
CONTAINS: WHEAT, SOY, MILK

U.S.
INSPECTED
AND PASSED BY
DEPARTMENT OF
AGRICULTURE
EST. 87

212 22 0137 ID367 42...

0 85239 22 1...

INTRODUCTION

Now more than ever, packaging has a huge opportunity to prove itself as a brand's most valuable consumer touchpoint. For designers, it's a time of newfound awareness of the power of design. This attention brings with it responsibilities for each of us to present and represent our talents in ways that build and establish permanence to design's valued role in business. In writing this book, John Silva and I set out to create a guide for designers that is also informative to the many other professionals involved in the process, providing understanding and value for all. Packaging requires the expertise of many disciplines: marketing, strategic planning, research, psychology, art, industrial design, graphic design, logistics, engineering, production, manufacturing, distribution, and retailing to name just a few. This complexity means package design doesn't happen in a vacuum. Many factors influence a final piece, and this book reflects that truth as we take you on the creative journey to successful packaging.

With the fragmentation of traditional advertising, due mainly to the overwhelming number of media delivery options, more companies are looking to a product's package to deliver the brand message to consumers directly. After all, every package is seen by 100 percent of a brand's consumers. As a result, the retail experience is in a constant state of evolution as brands and products are continually positioning themselves in new and innovative ways.

Humans are excited by new ideas and experiences. Whether we are searching for a product, surfing the Internet, or traveling to an unfamiliar country, we all enjoy the act of discovery. It is what drives and motivates change. Creativity is an act of discovery and is found by those individuals who push the boundaries within a profession.

As cultures evolve, so does the visual language that expresses this moment in time. As designers, we are creators and adopters of new aesthetic paradigms, shaping and molding human information. It has been proven in case study after case study in product categories from computers to soda that great design sells. If you look at these success stories closely, as we do in this book, you'll see that design is always founded on innovative positioning and solid, consistent brand strategy. This is what we mean by art plus science in packaging: the ability to take sophisticated research and analysis and convert it to visually stimulating design. This collaboration of opposites—rational science with emotional, artistic thinking—can and does make for unpredictable situations and solutions. How we manage them, and who is in charge of the process, can seriously affect the product outcome.

In this book, we analyze the steps and processes needed for success—from the preparation of strategic briefs through creative development to prepress and completion—every step has its purpose and value. During the creative journey, we give examples that provide inspiration as well as templates for your own triumphs.

Companies assessing package design firms look beyond creative talent; they seek designers with a real ability to understand human behavior and target consumers in a compelling, fresh, and entertaining way. This book provides the key.

~ Steven DuPuis

PACKAGING
EVOLUTION

Which came first—the product or the package?

PACKAGING is the Time Capsule of Our Being

What we consider a package—something that holds, protects, and stores its contents—occurs naturally, as in the protective covering of a banana, the cocoon of a butterfly, and an oyster, with its hidden treasure. These all perform the functions of a package. Humankind's creative curiosity has led to the adoption of many of nature's examples. In 100 B.C., the Chinese used sheets of treated mulberry bark to wrap food. Containers made from clay, shells, animal skins, and leaves functioned as they did in nature. As societies and cultures grew, communication and clarity became important; therefore, icons and words began to grace the surface of containers.

Changing Role

Evolving over time from basic utility to marketing vehicle, the simple package has become complex. It still functions, of course, but now it's made from a host of high-tech materials and has taken on unconventional forms and shapes. It features delivery systems such as pull-tops, self-cooling devices, biodegradable inks, and date codes that change color when expired. All of these innovations improve and expand on the functionality of the package while giving the manufacturer an edge over its competition.

Even the term *packaging* has evolved, from *package* (a container) to *packaging* (a container that has written communication about its specific contents). This transformation occurred in the nineteenth century and segued into the development of brands. Branding has grown to become the most important marketing tool, with packaging as its most ardent companion.

The evolution of packaging has played an important role in the advancement of humankind. Today many of us take for granted how products are brought to the shelf and how they are manufactured and packaged to protect against damage or spoilage. We now live in a society that looks beyond the functional aspects of packaging to how it makes one feel, look, and speak. Image has become the driving force behind packaging and branding. From utilitarian function to emotional billboard, the package now serves two masters: It hosts the brand, and it entices the potential buyer through inviting graphics and entertaining visuals. The functional qualities of packaging are seen through distinctive delivery systems of convenience and portability. Packages must keep up with consumers' changing lifestyles.

More Changes

In today's market, we could broaden our definition of *packaging* to include the packaging of entire brands, not just specific products. Leading companies such as Target, Nike, Whole Foods, and Starbucks are brands whose packaging extends to the entire retail experience. For them, the idea of packaging goes beyond the container to the total package of the store. This is a real brand experience. And it is the packaging of this brand experience that allows us to become enchanted and entertained. Consumers connect on a whole new level with the complete concept of packaging.

From the **BEGINNING**—A Walk Through the Packaging **TIMELINE**

Curiosity and creative spirit have made us challenge and improve our quality of life. Early quests to explore the world created a demand for goods. Trade routes brought spices, silks, scents, teas, coffee, wine, and chocolate—all of which had to be carried long distances. Economies grew and societies flourished based on the ability to transport goods around the world. This led to the establishment of monetary systems, giving value to products and services. The Egyptians developed glass and gave

us the first glass jars. Centuries later, glass-making techniques became a closely guarded Venetian trade secret. By the early 1600s, trade and commerce defined economies and ranked societies by their ability to manufacture, distribute, and store goods. Packaging played a pivotal role in the balance of power within Europe. Indeed, packaging as early as the sixteenth century shows that containers, bottles, and boxes were used to give a higher perceived value to all kinds of products. In 1795, the Napoleonic government of

France announced it would give a prize of 12,000 francs (about $2,500) to whoever could develop a way of preserving food for long periods. If accomplished, this would give France a military advantage by giving troops the ability to move quickly into new territory without the worry of food preparation. Nicolas Appert worked on developing an airtight seal on glass jars, perfected it by 1810, and was granted a patent in that same year. However, in England, a patent was granted for the tin can, which also preserved food in an airtight

1500 B.C.	100 B.C.	1798	1810	1817

EGYPT First glass jars	**CHINA** Sheets of treated mulberry bark were used to wrap foods.	**GERMANY** Lithography was invented by ALOIS SENEFELDER.	**ENGLAND** PETER DURAND got a patent for devising the sealed round tin can.	**ENGLAND** First cardboard box

environment. The English had mobility in addition to preserved food, and so they defeated Napoleon at Waterloo.

Time and again, the transportation and storage of food became a strategic advantage among nations. Tin cans were used in the U.S. Civil War before they were available to the public, and they ultimately allowed the population to urbanize. Once again, packages changed society.

Icons of Trust and Safety

The industrial revolution of the nineteenth century brought with it the mass movement of people from farms to cities. People left their small communities, where they knew their neighbors and their local grocer, for large, unfamiliar cities. They also left behind their farming jobs, replacing them with wage-earning factory work. This created an environ-ment in which packaging could flourish. Along with packaging came the rise in popularity of brands like Borden, Quaker, Campbell's, and Coca-Cola.

Early advertising played a role in giving these brands personality and assuring the public of their fresh, sterile, germ-free qualities. This resulted in a trust that could not be matched with the dirty and unsanitary store environments of the 1800s. The can, bottle, and box adorned with memorable graphics were recognizable icons of trust and safety.

In 1858, New York had a massive milk contamination problem from cows too close to the city. Gale Borden was not affected because his cows were over 100 miles (161 km) away. Borden Dairy's canned condensed-milk product could be shipped easily and kept fresh without refrigeration. Most of all, it was seen as safe. Borden was quick to see an opportunity and so positioned his product as clean and pure. Consumers came to trust his products, feeling they were much safer than fresh milk.

Events like these caused consumer confidence to turn to packaged products for reasons of trust and quality. The huge demand fueled innovation. One invention that had a huge impact, especially on the popularity of all kinds of canned goods, was the creation of the can opener in 1865. It was at this time that canned goods sales soared.

1844	1858	1865	1866	1867

ENGLAND First commercial paper bags	**USA** GALE BORDEN developed condensed milk.	**ENGLAND** The can opener was invented.	**USA** Early use of branding on packaging— SMITH BROTHERS cough drops	**USA** First printed metal containers were made for DR. LYONS

History Continues—
The **MARKETING** of **PACKAGING**

The late 1800s saw advances in automation, printing, transportation, and materials, allowing packaged goods to be offered to all economic groups and shipped around the world. Technology enabled mass production to grow and the prices of goods to decrease, triggering the beginning of a consuming, disposable society. It was then that the word *consumer* was coined.

Henry Parsons Crowell, founder of The Quaker Oats Company, was one of the first to use what we view now as modern marketing methods. Like marketers today, he assessed the environment and the potential consumer. He looked at what was deemed successful at the time, primarily patent medicine containers adorned with figures of doctors, which gave buyers a sense of trust. He also heard of the bronze statue of William Penn being placed atop Philadelphia's City Hall. Crowell's Quaker figure was quite possibly inspired by these examples, along with images drawn from the Quaker faith. His packaging also featured the word *pure*, which addressed the food safety concerns of the period. What made Quaker unique was Crowell's intuitive understanding of marketing, specifically the power of branding, which he consistently implemented throughout his campaigns.

Crowell understood the principle of creating desire by developing advertising that said, "Is it worth trying?" He also ran editorial stories that spoke of the health qualities of his product. To create demand, he went about the country giving

1916	1930	1937	1950	1970
USA Coca-Cola introduces its distinctively shaped bottle.	MASSACHUSETTS Clarence Birdseye begins retail sales of frozen food products.	OKLAHOMA The first shopping cart inspired by two folding chairs was born.	NEBRASKA As frozen food sales grow, Swanson introduces the first TV dinner.	CALIFORNIA The recycling symbol identifies packages made from recyclable fibers.

away small boxes of the product. On the back of the package, he printed recipes and emphasized ease of preparation. He used the Quaker image on everything from packages to billboards to advertising. In all, he developed an integrated branding and marketing program that is still valid in today's marketplace.

Urbanization and Industrialization

A significant shift occurred in retail in the early twentieth century. A change in the grocer's role as product gatekeeper. Before this time, consumers purchased goods at counters behind which the grocery clerk stood. The buyer told the grocer what she wanted and he would hand it to her. This gave little opportunity for customers to involve themselves with the package prior to purchase. The develop-

ment of self-serve stores changed all that.

New grocery stores had aisles where consumers selected at will what they wanted. They could pick up products and interact with them before the purchase. This revolution allowed brands to compete, unobstructed, with the consumer. It also created an environment where a variety of competitive products were shelved next to each other. Packaging now became the silent salesman, competing for consumer attention.

Thus the role of packaging evolved into a vital marketing tool in selling products. This eventually created ancillary industries, with consumer research, branding, industrial design, and graphic design all becoming well-established commercial professions. Today, increased competition within matured retail markets has resulted in advances in market strategy, behav-

ioral science, structural materials, and creative design combined with innovative technology to offer us a world of ever-changing retail experiences.

1973   1974   1977   1980   2007

OHIO
The first bar code appears on a pack of Wrigley's gum.

KENTUCKY
The stay-on tab is invented and introduced by Falls City Brewing Co.

USA
The more impermeable PETE plastic is used to make soda bottles.

TEXAS
Whole Foods opens its first natural foods supermarket.

USA
Al Gore alerts us to global warming, making us rethink.

Brands **EVOLVE** and **DIFFERENTIATE** to Create Choice

On cluttered shelves with lots of commodity products, the package serves as the lone tangible element to position and differentiate a brand and product from its competitors. It also plays an important role as the final communication device before purchase. Advertising creates awareness of and desire for the product. But once the consumer is standing in the aisle, he is tempted by the many similar products vying for his attention. Without the package, the product is indistinguishable from its competitors.

The two piles of cornflakes pictured below are from different manufacturers, but who can tell which is which? If one is selling for more money, the package must convince the buyer the product is worth the extra cost. Packaging, and the image it carries, serves as that motivator. It is at this point that branding plays an important part in choice; it helps consumers make decisions by saying, "Trust me, you know me, you have always had great results with me, use me again."

Connection to Brands

In the late 1950s, retail environments were changing, with the introduction of supermarkets giving rise to an explosion of new products, cluttering the marketplace, and causing the science of branding to grow into a well-established industry. The psychology of consumer behavior, buying habits, and product loyalties were studied and analyzed, giving marketers and designers new insights into what drives a purchase. Terms such as *brand personality* and *brand essence* were used to explain new methodologies and disciplines that were adopted. This made way for branding and packaging to weave itself into the cultural landscape of society. Coca-Cola is a good example: Its early ad campaign is credited with creating the current look of Santa Claus, while its bottle is one of the most recognizable shapes in the world. Today the Coca-Cola *brand*, valued at $68 billion (£34 billion), is worth much more than its manufacturing plants.

Population growth from baby boomers, and the expansive growth of urban sprawl, made supermarkets the retail location of choice for consumers. The new stores offered thousands of products

in wide, brightly lit aisles. Marketers were challenged to make their products jump off the shelf. Innovations such as freeze-dried food, aluminum pouches, frozen TV dinners, and plastic bottles allowed products to have a longer shelf life and provided convenience to consumers. Design made advances in structural styles, typography, and printing processes. A brand's point of difference, positioning, and personality became distinguishable attributes through the use of unique typography, color, and graphic elements. We saw a rise in character personalities used to represent or endorse the brand. Betty Crocker, Uncle Ben, Mr. Clean, the Jolly Green Giant, and Tony the Tiger all gave consumers the comfort of a personality presenting the product. The human connection is strong, and therefore today these brands still use these characters.

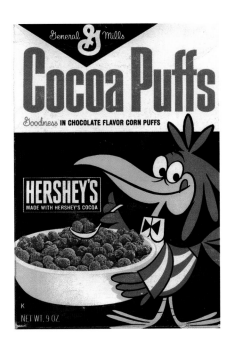

Top: Early cereal boxes show that marketers were faced with some of the same challenges we have today with benefit claims and promotional offerings. Within the category, promotions have long been a strong driver in drawing moms and kids to product brands. We still see this today, however, more focus is placed on product experience and appetite appeal.

Right: Walter Landor, middle, was an early adopter of mock shelf sets which he had installed in the Landor office. These sets were used in evaluating designs and for consumer research.

The **POWER** of Packaging for the Brand

In the mid-1900s, manufacturers saw the value in developing marketing strategies for their products. Many changed their focus and developed brands and packages with such effectiveness that consumers saw them as one and the same. What was Coke without its bottle? Or ketchup without the Heinz label? Or Campbell's soup without the red label? Some products became so synonymous with their brand names that their names were the very words used to describe the entire category of competitors—Thermos, Kleenex, Band-Aid, and Pop-Tarts, to name a few.

Increased Competition

Brand image was developed in the early 1960s as a way to further differentiate products from their increasing competition. Packaging was, and still is, the perfect communication vehicle to showcase brand image.

In today's cluttered marketplace, packaging continues to evolve and become even more sophisticated. Research shows that different brand images delivered via packaging appeal to different consumer demographic segments. Market research into consumer behaviors, along with demographic and psychographic analysis, are all used to position brands and refine product packaging. The resulting designs catch consumers' eyes. Packaging can be so strong that it makes a brand instantly recognizable.

1914

1956

1921

1968

Left: The Morton Salt girl with umbrella has been updated and modernized with changing times and styles, but through its transformation, the image stayed true to its equities.

Right: The iconic Quaker brand keeps true to its heritage, evolving over time but never losing sight of established equities. Consumer conveniences, along with nutrition and lifestyle changes are adopted, but the brand retains the core design elements that are so recognizable.

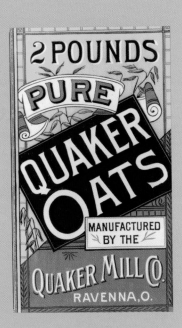

Walter Landor (above), Henry Dreyfuss (top, right), and Saul Bass (right), are three of the significant branding and packaging pioneers in the field of design. Their strategic approach and creative excellence earned the respect of clients and propelled the professional brand design industry forward.

PIONEERS of Branding and Packaging Design

In the second quarter of the twentieth century, advertising matured into a viable industry that flourished because of the wealth of new brands and products. Packaging design also grew within this environment as companies faced increased competition. Fashion designers, artists, engineers, and architects were some of the early pioneers to shape and define this creative discipline. Designers such as Raymond Loewy, Ben Nash, Henry Dreyfuss, and John Vassos pioneered and set the stage for industrial design and packaging design to grow and become a valuable business asset.

Brand Design Emerges

Decades later, strategic creative firms emerged—including Saul Bass, Primo Angeli, Deskey Associates, Landor Associates, and Gerstman + Meyers—which defined and shaped the structure of today's brand design agency. The term used to describe a packaging design firm varies, as does the products or services of each. The positioning of a firm is based on its image and the services it offers. The firms mentioned above were seen as strategic in that they understood marketing and how to apply business thinking to creative solutions. Their success was in their ability to unite marketing strategy and artistic expression in innovative solutions that garnered results for their clients.

Through the years, design, in its application to business, has had many names. Much of the variation is in response to the ever-evolving role design plays within companies and popular culture. The terms *commercial art, graphic design, visual communication, corporate communication, corporate identities, brand consultants, brand design,* and *package design* have all graced the business cards of well-known designers.

Design Reflects Culture

For all designers, whatever they call their specialty, it's key to be attuned to events that can cause shifts in thought, as these occurrences will give rise to new styles and vocabularies. For example, the launch of Russia's Sputnik spacecraft in the 1960s caused a complete change in style and helped usher in the modern era. Sleek, streamlined shapes were desired. Loewy noted the cultural change, revitalizing the Coke bottle to give it a more contemporary styling. Designers must strive to create work that speaks to current cultural environments while stretching boundaries into new sensory experiences.

"It can't be stressed enough that in order to produce great graphics, you have to have a good product and a good client capable of making decisions."

Primo Angeli

INNOVATION in Packaging Generates Consumer Demand

Innovation is vital to the success of a brand's life. All aspects of the product/package and marketing lifecycle need innovation—from media formats, promotions, structural containers, computer technology, manufacturing, and design styles to printing processes. Continued evolution is the creative glue that perpetually involves consumers with the brand.

Today we see innovation as a key driver in developing brand awareness and loyalty. Consumers want to be entertained. In addition, they have short attention spans and get bored easily. Brands must constantly evolve and reinvent themselves. Gone are the days in which brands can stagnate but persist. Change is now part of every brand's DNA.

Consumers are constantly being drawn to new and different products. The change in a product, however, must be relevant to the essence of the brand and consistent with consumers' expectations and desires. Evolution doesn't mean radically abandoning equities but rather implementing what will keep the consumer relationship fresh and alive. Heinz ketchup, for instance, has an iconic mark that is valuable, so the innovative changes were placed within the label's distinctive shield shape. In a special promotion, pithy sayings such as "Starving for the Spotlight?" and "Want a Taste of Fame?" were placed on the label, sparking a quick laugh from consumers and giving new life to the Heinz brand. In contrast, Mountain Dew has more license to change their image due to the brand's rebellious personality and young consumer base. Here the expectation for change is so great the product used an aluminum bottle to showcase multiple styles.

Markets, and the way consumers receive information, have changed, leaving the package a major marketing tool. Packages have become three-dimensional ads for brands. Money is being redirected from advertising budgets to packaging. Money is being spent at the shelf level through innovation, design, promotions, and packaging materials, all in hopes of developing engaging brand experiences. We now see packages that change color when they are hot or cold as well as ones that light up and talk. Their innovative functionality continues even after purchase, becoming a pleasant decoration or providing an efficient delivery system and then moving on to easy disposal or recycling. The lifespan of a package is now evaluated by consumers and seen as part of the total brand experience.

Top: Artistic expression was used to build brand experience and connect young consumers to Mountain Dew, designed by Pepsi Design Group.

Left: Structure plays an important role in creating differentiation and value. For Axe, by Just Blue Design, it was a way to connect to its consumer base.

Technology markets have had to constantly develop new and innovative experiences. Turner Duckworth gave the Motorola cell phone a space-age look that allowed the product to feel new, special, and high-tech.

The ice-capped mountains on the Coors Light label turns blue when the bottle is chilled to the optimum drinking temperature for beer.

Creating **PREFERENCES** Through Package Design

Packaging is an essential component in our culture. More than a container, a bag, a box, or a bottle, it tells stories and makes promises in an attempt to win trust. It presents and promotes, informs, and instructs. A package's eye-catching graphics and messages make all kinds of products desirable, sellable, understandable, memorable, and entertaining. With commoditization has come positioning and the targeting of specific consumers who look through the sea of choices to find the one they see as specifically meant for them.

Without the package, products may be similar to, if not the same as, their competitors. Water is a good example: You can't change the product, which is always clear and hard to distinguish by taste. Also, it is readily available, so positioning and image are critical. The examples shown vary in price from $1.25 to $7.00 (£0.6 to £3.4) per bottle. Here is where design and marketing must work their magic to convince a buyer to pay more for a commodity product. In each example, they are catering to different buyers who value and believe in their brand.

Moment of Truth

In 2005, the *Wall Street Journal* reported on multinational manufacturing giant Procter & Gamble's concept of the First Moment of Truth (or FMOT, pronounced "EFF-mot"), writing, "Procter & Gamble believes shoppers make up their mind

about a product in about the time it takes to read this [sentence]." Essentially, in the first three to seven seconds after a shopper encounters a product on a store shelf, marketers have the best chance of turning a browser into a buyer. The way to do this is by appealing to consumers' senses, values, and emotions. Of course, the way to make this appeal is through packaging and other point-of-sale devices.

In her book The *Substance of Style*, *New York Times* columnist Virginia Postrel comments that, increasingly, consumers make product decisions based on how a product makes them feel. Going further, she observes the power of design to help elicit feelings. "In a crowded marketplace," notes Postrel, "aesthetics is often the only way to make a product stand out."

Packaging Preferences

Let's face it, consumers today are a moving target. Marketers get only a few seconds to attract them, hold their attention, and turn casual browsers into serious buyers. Many factors contribute to maneuvering consumers into a retail environment, but once they are there, it's the job of packaging to prompt sales. A package not only delivers the product to the consumer, it brings the consumer to the brand.

Here are ways design can affect consumer's preferences:

- Attract the eye with greater impact on the shelf.
- Cause the belief that a product is better than its competitors.
- Provide clear and relevant information.
- Appeal directly to the senses.
- Link consumers to communities.

BRAND IMAGE PARADIGM

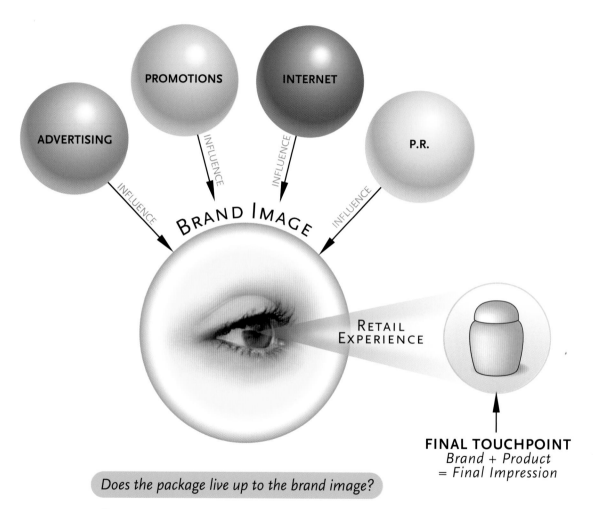

PROMOTIONS

INTERNET

ADVERTISING

P.R.

INFLUENCE

INFLUENCE

INFLUENCE

INFLUENCE

BRAND IMAGE

RETAIL EXPERIENCE

FINAL TOUCHPOINT
*Brand + Product
= Final Impression*

Does the package live up to the brand image?

CONSIDER THIS:
- *75 percent of a purchase decision is made at the shelf.*
- *100 percent of your buyers see the package.*

No other form of communication can claim such impact.

Packaging's Role Keeps **CHANGING**

Packaging design is an exciting field that continues to evolve. More than just devices that enclose and protect products for distribution, storage, sale, and use, packages work hard to attract and convince consumers to purchase. The role of packaging continues to grow and change. New innovations in materials, manufacturing, and printing are developed as technology advances in the marketplace in response to changing consumer needs and lifestyles. Watch for packaging to take on additional responsibility in marketing to consumers.

More and more brand managers and marketers are recognizing the strong effect great packaging can have on purchase intent. Not surprisingly, we see store brands or private-label products embracing new trends and taking risks more readily than the large global brands. This has given rise to consumers involving themselves with store brands more often, as they feel the packaging is entertaining and engaging. Knowing that design has made the difference is something all designers can use to argue in favor of using package design as an effective tool that can help boost the bottom line.

Because corporations have seen how creative packaging and brand identity have positively impacted the sales and growth of certain products, design is now being considered a real player in marketing. Designers must step up and articulate their designs' results, not just talk about the wonderful aesthetics, in order to capture these new opportunities.

Advertising

Advertising is public communication, paid for and controlled by a brand that is distributed via a variety of media delivery methods, including television, radio, movies, the Internet, newspapers and magazines, and outdoor vehicles like billboards and bus shelters. Its primary role is to draw attention, spark awareness, and create desire.

Promotions

With a primary goal of furthering a brand's popularity, promotions can be "above the line," by communicating paid messages through the media, or "below the line," by means of sponsorship, product placement, endorsements, and public relations. Promotions also work to increase sales, boost acceptance, enhance brand image, and create trial.

Packaging

Packaging is primarily the containing device for products, but it also works as part of the marketing mix of tools by delivering graphic communications and brand messages along with the product itself directly into the hands of the buyer. It delivers the brand idea.

Proving Our Value: **MEASURING** Package Design's Return on Investment

An Interview with Rob Wallace, *Director of Strategy, Wallace Church, Inc., New York, NY*

Q. *What is your background?*

A. I have over 20 years in package design, and I'm the director of strategy for Wallace Church, Inc., a strategic brand identity and package design firm. I'm a frequent contributor to magazines such as *Fast Company, Design Management Journal,* and *Package Design.*

Q. *What do you focus on in your writing about package design?*

A. I have tried to spread the gospel of package design's preeminent role in communicating the brand's core identity, its emotional essence, and its primary connection to consumers. We've shown that, if brought into the strategic marketing process early and given the chance to set the visual platform for all brand communications, package design can affect unprecedented results.

Q. *Hasn't it always been advertising that leads the way, not packaging?*

A. I cut my teeth at Grey Advertising. I've seen how potent advertising can be. Unfortunately, that's not the case

today. I can't state strongly enough that the power of traditional advertising vehicles is eroding. They are no longer effective in the way they were. For most consumer products, we believe package design is the single most sales-effective and cost-efficient marketing tool. Many corporations have elevated the term *package design* to *brand identity design.* Smart corporations are taking advantage of the increased role packaging can play in their brand's success.

Good packaging can promote a fantastic level of interest in a product. It can go beyond loyalty; great packages can create brand advocates. It is the single most compelling vehicle a marketer can use to connect with consumers—100 percent of a product's buyers interact with its package.

Q. *Are corporations recognizing the power of package design?*

A. Many corporations still don't engage in brand identity until well after brand strategy has been established, and only a precious few actually validate results

that brand identity generates. Because designers have talked to their clients' executive management in terms of creativity and not process, they are not addressing an audience that believes, "If you can't measure it, you can't manage it." As designers, we need to start speaking about return on investment (ROI) when we talk about packaging.

Q. *Is packaging ROI possible?*

A. Yes, I am confident that ROI is real and measurable. We've done it at Wallace Church in conjunction with statisticians from Northeastern University for some of our clients. Unfortunately the results are confidential, so I can't share specifics, but we have been able to obtain empirical proof of a design's direct impact on the bottom line. Handled properly, this information points directly to design's value. We are working on bringing our methodologies into industrywide practice.

Q. *What are some of the ways designers can talk about a quantifiable ROI?*

A. Talk about efficacy. Research shows that well over two-thirds of consumer product purchase decisions are made at point of sale. In some categories, impulse purchasing at shelf accounts for 85 percent of sales. It is quite evident that brand identity and package design drive this all-important dynamic.

In terms of recall, also known as *"brand equity"* cross-category studies show that in unaided awareness tests consumers remember more about the package than they do about advertising or promotions. Hundreds of equity studies confirm that consumers recall the color of a package first, the shape or structure second, and the style of a brand's logo third. This proves the most recognized components are design-related.

Also address impressions. One hundred percent of a brand's current and potential audience is exposed to a product at retail when encountering its package. A package's influence continues well after purchase is made.

Q. *Can packaging ROI really be measured?*

A. It's an evolving concept. In the past, measurements have been largely subjective. As we move forward, technology will allow corporations to track data from all aspects of a product's lifecycle. We will be able to look at various data from inventory through sales and analyze the impact of whole brand communication programs to evaluate ROI. It's definitely something creatives and brand managers agree would be very useful in the fight for the budgets and resources needed to optimize the brand identity process.

Q. *What does the future hold for brand identity and ROI?*

A. In the end, it's all about brand identity being involved in the first five minutes of marketing, not as an afterthought. Designers need to understand the marketing process and how their decisions affect their client's business. Clients need to understand that brand identity design belongs as the cornerstone of all their marketing efforts.

Go to Rob Wallace's "Notes on Design" at http://blog.sessions.edu/author/rob-wallace/ for more on ROI.

Wallace Church has designed value-driven packaging for brands such as Ken's Light Accent Dressing, and Heinz.

THE ART AND SCIENCE OF
PACKAGE DESIGN

Bridging the gap between business strategy and design

Creating the **RATIONAL** and **EMOTIONAL** Connection

"If you eliminate the emotional guiding factors, it's impossible for people to make decisions in daily life." *The University of Rochester School of Medicine*

Every day, we are faced with making both rational and emotional decisions. People are drawn to the rational because it is explainable, measurable, and finite. However, rational thinking does not always play into consumer behavior. Sometimes it's all about emotions. Whether you are a package designer or a product marketer, it's critical to understand both the emotional and the rational drivers that affect product success in the marketplace. To do this, you must examine the influences of both the left and the right brain.

Right- or Left-Brain Thinking

Although the two sides of the brain are similar in appearance, the function of each cerebral hemisphere is different. The left side governs linear reasoning, rational and analytical thoughts, while the right side deals with holistic reasoning, the emotional, and the artistic. This is a broad generalization, but research does support the notion of specialized areas of brain function. Apparently individuals do have a preferred method of approaching the world—rationally or emotionally, using left- or right-brain thinking. By recognizing the existence of "right-brained people" and "left-brained people," theory becomes practice when objectives to satisfy both or either are woven into the design process. This is especially significant in the early planning and strategy phases of development.

Packaging Calls for Both

Design taps into both modes of thinking to make lasting connections with consumers. Successful package design plays both sides of the fence by integrating left-brain strategies with right-brain creative vision. Although these two forces often seem at odds, in the hands of a skilled team, design provides a balance that motivates purchase. A package can be pleasing to the eye while offering precise product information, for example.

Effective design is a vital ingredient for building successful brands. Here, again, the impact of both right-brain and left-brain factors is seen. All too often, strategic issues, operational concerns, logistical tactics, and entrenched marketing attitudes can overshadow design, cutting off its full potential to contribute to the bottom line. Design can be a powerful emotional language, but it's also a highly effective means of clarifying and organizing messages. That is why it is key to translate scientific knowledge, marketing research, and other left-brained pursuits into unique right-brain solutions. The services of a skilled package designer are not purely about creating a beautiful design; they're about an intuitive understanding of what motivates consumers to purchase a product or service.

seeks answers · examines and questions

values explanations · values observation

controlled and · spontaneous
mechanical   and intuitive

literal and explicit · metaphysical and organic

works step-by-step · sees the whole at once

LEFT SIDE OF THE BRAIN: WORDS

The brain's left side governs the rational
and analytical. It's the side of the brain that
makes us logical, sequential, and objective.

RIGHT SIDE OF THE BRAIN: PICTURES

The right side processes the emotional and
artistic. This brain's hemisphere causes us
to be holistic, random, and synthesizing.
Right-brain focus is emotive and creative.

Creating Real and Lasting Client-to-Customer **CONNECTIONS**

Using the Art and Science of Package Design

People are bombarded with countless marketing messages every day. With the average retailer stocking 40,000 products, it's no wonder consumers have learned to tune out and filter. Product parity and price competition have led marketers to seek new directions for differentiation. Designers and their clients are seeking new ways of communicating with and ultimately connecting to consumers.

Packaging keeps evolving, and so do the people who create and market the products. Technology has changed how we work while retailing has changed the way we buy packaging. Lifestyle and value shifts will always influence the face of packaging. It is a reflection of our culture; it defines us, just as we define it.

Brand Authenticity

Consumers are hypersensitive and overexposed to design, so much so that they are critical of its manifestation. They involve themselves with what keeps them interested and entertained. Today companies must be honest in their endeavors because consumers are skepti-

cal. Issues of obesity, health, nutrition, origin, sustainability, freshness, and safety are all critical concerns. While packaging designers often want to go simple to avoid visual clutter, consumers want to learn more from the package.

Inherent to all companies that produce a product is the constant quest to innovate for a competitive edge. To add value and convenience, many companies launch new brands or extend established brands into an already confusing marketplace. Once introduced into the market, these often fail to interest the consumer. Was the product a bad idea? Or was it poorly presented to the consumer?

Consumer Behavior

Understanding how consumers experience a brand and its products is the secret to successful marketing. After all, the brand is more than a well-designed logo. It has personality and an inherent level of approachability. People gravitate toward brands like they choose their friends. This connection requires more than a pleasing aesthetic. A brand

designed to connect hits the consumer on an emotional level. The package may be silent, but through design it triggers senses and an emotional buying decision. Packaging also must appeal to the rational and factual requirements consumers have, proving the product is also the logical choice. These connections are necessary when launching a new brand or invigorating one with a legacy.

Product Differentiation

Designers and marketers need to realize they are not just selling products; they are telling stories through packaging. Package design is the visual expression of the brand's soul. Used effectively, packaging can define, build, and entertain consumers. However, to develop effective packaging that lives up to its potential, both art and science must be considered.

Packaging connects target audiences to brands. Using design, these products are able to attract and appeal on an emotional level that persuades consumers to purchase. Gazer soft drinks by Real Pro, St. Germain liqueur by Sandstrom, and Moravian cookies by Shapiro Walker Design all make the right connections.

Packaging Design **TEAM JOURNEY**

The team is the heart of any project. If the heart is not pumping correctly, the body loses energy, becomes fatigued and sluggish, and can die. Having the smartest and most talented people on your team is no guarantee of success.

Collaborative Discovery

Relationship is an ever-present word in our industry, and for good reason. The packaging design process is highly collaborative. Designers and clients are on a journey of discovery together. For clients, the creative journey is just as important as the final destination or design solution. If they have a bad experience with your team, even if they have a fantastic end product, chances are you won't be hired again. Just as we speak about brand experience within a retail setting, our own brand is viewed and evaluated the same way.

Client Designer Team

Whether you are a sole proprietor working with a small client, a large design firm working with a Fortune 500 company, or an in-house design department working with an internal marketing department, the relationship between you and the client grows and is nurtured through mutual respect. In each

of these working arrangements, team synergy is essential. First and foremost, roles and responsibilities, along with team objectives, must be set to form the foundation for ultimate success. All too often, projects are started without these basic principles. Creative briefs are lacking in ownable content, positioning is not unique, or the objectives are not clear—all of which lead package design teams down blind paths.

With mutual goals intact, teams can work together to achieve great solutions. Having bright talent that can look at problems from a variety of viewpoints is imperative, but even more important is how well team members work *together*.

Improving the Odds

If you have a dysfunctional team, it is virtually impossible to reach success. In these situations, you need to look for ways to improve the team's dynamics. Is the problem bad chemistry? Personality clashes? Understand that conflict can be a good thing, as long as it's achieved with respect for others. Conflict can lead to new creative ideas.

Within any given team situation, each person must understand the game plan for the project. Who is making the decisions? How far do they want to push the project? This should be

in the brief. The larger the group, the more room there is for watering down a good idea. Designers must keep the team on track by reviewing and clearly communicating objectives in relation to the creative. Large or small, teams need good leaders with focused goals.

The Russian design firm IMA created the packaging for a new line of "cosmeceutical" body care products for Eastern European markets. Simple, clean architecture provides a visual point of difference and effectively blends the worlds of cosmetics and medicine. The product exceeded sales expectations without additional advertising resources.

THE PACKAGING TEAM
—Collaboration Between Art & Science—

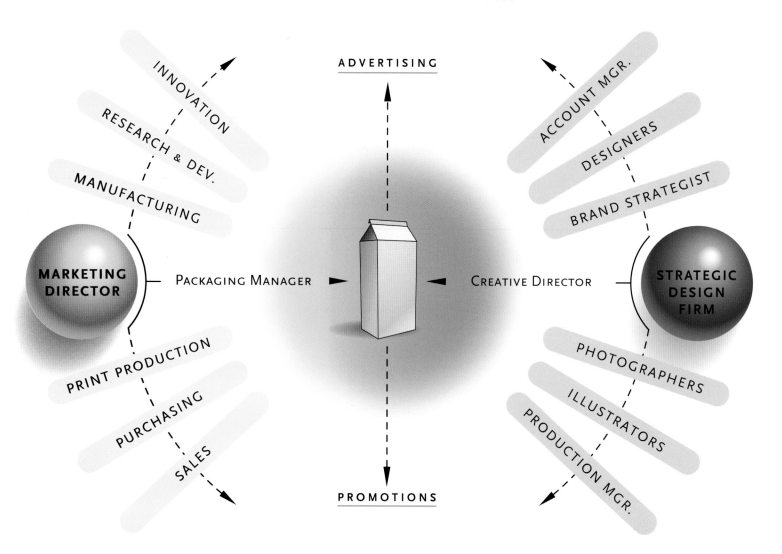

ADVERTISING

INNOVATION
RESEARCH & DEV.
MANUFACTURING

ACCOUNT MGR.
DESIGNERS
BRAND STRATEGIST

MARKETING DIRECTOR

Packaging Manager

Creative Director

STRATEGIC DESIGN FIRM

PRINT PRODUCTION
PURCHASING
SALES

PHOTOGRAPHERS
ILLUSTRATORS
PRODUCTION MGR.

PROMOTIONS

A broad array of talent, skill, and knowledge is required for the development of any package. Many people and factors contribute to a product's success.

The chart, (left), identifies many of them. Marketers occupy a central role and ultimately are held responsible for the success of a brand or product. They must have a keen sense of timing, consumer insight, and intuition to launch or revitalize products for their respective brands.

Within a design firm, the creative director plays a key role in fully understanding the brand and the products it represents. He or she is the leader, guiding both client and design teams to targeted solutions. The creative director must possess an innate ability to evaluate consumer behavior, project goals, as well as applicable aesthetic and cultural trends and the further ability to turn this knowledge into creative solutions that are stimulating and effective for the market.

Top-Down
STEWARDSHIP

When DuPuis looks for a creative who really stands out and has what it takes to do great package design, we look for talent, instinct, and soul. The practical skills and techniques needed to apply a designer's talent and instinct can be taught. Even with many working skills and knowledge of graphic applications, a person without creative soul cannot learn instinct and do outstanding design. Creative stewardship comes from the inside out, not the outside in.

Similarly, true creativity, instinct, marketing savvy, and talent are the wellspring for all brand inception and success. But without the top-down flow of strategy and vision, techniques and teachable processes are nothing more than commodities that are easily misused and easily replaced. Bottom-up stewardship is not possible; it is a flawed concept in every way.

DuPuis partners with clients in the brand innovation and development stages to establish the vital beginnings of top-down creative stewardship. By doing so, we ensure that what a brand embodies does not get lost during its inception, creation, implementation, production, duplication, and expansion.

Top-down stewardship reaches beyond strategy and design into the most remote steps of execution. It requires a team of experts that live and speak to a brand's purpose while wielding a powerful command of back-end processes, from production through distribution, that can make or break a brand's impact.

Without visionary leadership, package designers can't do their best work. Clearly articulated creative briefs certainly set the tone and work as a great foundation to any packaging initiative. However, it takes top-down stewardship—belief in the creative team, the design process, and the resulting creative solution, coupled with the ability to champion these and advocate effectively—which makes all the difference.

The **VALUE** of Package Design

An Interview with Terry Schwartz, *Director of Brand Design, ConAgra Foods Inc., Omaha, NE*

Q. *As the Senior Director of Brand Design, what is your role at ConAgra?*

A. My role is two-fold. First, it is my responsibility to create or have the vision for how design can influence the success of ConAgra Foods' brands. Secondly, for each brand, my team and I are asked to identify what opportunities exist for a specific marketing and design problem —on a project-by-project basis.

Q. *How do you view branding in its relationship to packaging?*

A. Branding is the expression of a brand —how it appears and is expressed across all the customer and consumer communication channels. One application of that brand expression is on the package.

Q. *In the marketing mix, what value does packaging play?*

A. Every part of the marketing mix has value and is important. But the package is the only vehicle that is considered alongside its competitors and is evaluated by the consumer at the point when they use and experience the brand. It most closely reflects the brand and what it stands for or promises.

Q. *What makes a successful package design?*

A. We believe there are four criteria that help to make a package successful: First, it must be consistent with the brand positioning and what the brand stands for—the design should express the brand story accurately. The second aspect of a successful package is that the design is relevant to the specific consumer the brand is targeting. Third, the package has to be clearly differentiated from the other options available to the consumer. And lastly, the design has to be well-integrated with the other communication vehicles. The brand will be expressed online, in advertising, in-store, etc, so a package is only successful if it works effectively with these other communication vehicles in a unified way.

Q. *What do you look for in hiring a packaging design firm?*

A. This is difficult because there are many excellent design agencies, and selecting an agency is a very important decision. Three elements influence our agency selection: First, a design firm needs to be a strategic problem solver. Many designers talk about doing this, but not everyone is actually successful at doing it consistently. We look for designers that understand

that design is a business-building strategy that demands that we approach it in a deliberate and strategic way. Secondly, we look for firms that have an intuitive creative capability. Certain firms simply have a greater ability to create engaging, persuasive, appealing design. Lastly, there needs to be solid chemistry between us and the agency—which is a little hard to define, but is important none-the-less. We need to respect each other. We need to be candid and be willing to listen to each other. We need to be partners in developing outstanding solutions.

Q. *What do you see as the biggest challenge for designers?*

A. The dynamics inside a corporate environment are very complex. There are many priorities and a constantly shifting balance of demands. This dynamic is the most difficult for us to communicate to our agencies and for the agencies to truly understand. The result of this is agencies periodically have a hard time adjusting to those shifting demands, leading the creative process in the context of those challenges, and coming out the other end with a design solution that meets the demands of the business.

Q. If you could change one thing within the branding and packaging industry what would it be?

A. If I had that kind of influence, I'd like to see greater integration of what happens on the package with the other customer and consumer communication elements. I'd like to see the design for our brands be more holistic and unified. When a brand is well integrated, then all elements are more effective (including packaging)— and the brand benefits more. Some of our brands do an outstanding job of that. Others can do better.

Q. What is the single biggest obstacle you see with package design?

A. I think the environment that our brands compete in is very complex and therefore filled with a variety of challenges. But one problem that we consistently see is a lack of a strong creative vision. That vision must come from the brand team, (my staff, marketing, R&D, etc), in order to stimulate the creative process. When that doesn't happen, the effectiveness of the final solution can suffer. On a more executional level, another challenge is the desire and request to put too much information on our packaging.

We typically want to say many more things than the consumer is interested in hearing. The result is the information that could influence their decision to buy a brand is more difficult to find and, in fact, may not be seen. It is a classic example of less is more.

The packaging for three of ConAgra Foods' major brands, Healthy Choice and Reddi wip by laga, and Slim Jim by Thompson Design Group, reflects each product line's positioning and promises.

Working with BIG BRANDS
VS. SMALL BRANDS

"You now have to decide what image you want for your brand. Image means personality. Products, like people, have personalities, and they can make or break them in the marketplace." *David Ogilvy, (called the "father of advertising")*

The fundamentals are the same, whether working for a large brand or a small brand, but the complexity and risk associated with large brands can alter the design development process. Large brands have established equities and brand loyalties that represent a huge part of their income.

More Complexity

Understanding consumers' behavior, and how a particular brand integrates into their life, is key to designing or identifying graphic changes for a design revitalization, especially in a big brand. Once the proper evaluation and observations have been done, a strategy can be developed.

Working under these analytical conditions is not for every designer. Different skill sets and expertise are required when working on large brands. Specifically, designers need to have a deep knowledge of branding and its effect on consumer buying habits. To serve a megabrand, a design firm needs a team of experts dedicated to evaluating trends and changes in the marketplace. These firms typically offer services outside of design, including strategic planning, market research, and brand analysis. As a result of the added complexity of large brand design programs, design firms typically charge higher fees.

More Flexibility

Conversely, small brands, if not owned by large companies, are much more adaptable, allowing them to reposition more quickly, and with less risk. Design, in these situations, is used as a strategic tool. Small brands are more easily able to capture new trends in the marketplace. Also, innovations in structure and printing processes can be launched faster due to smaller volumes. Layers within these organizations are much flatter, resulting in faster approval processes, typically with fewer changes. The downside to working on a smaller brand is often more limited budgets and lower compensation to the designer.

We see private-label or store brands taking advantage of big brands' weaknesses through innovative design. Because of this phenomenon, we see consumers becoming more engaged with their new fresh looks. The successful use of design as a point of differentiation is working to convince the big brands that design is, indeed, a valuable tool.

Right: Boutique brands like Amy's, designed by Ray Honda Designs, have different challenges and opportunities than a major international brand like Knorr Ragu by Design Bridge.

Small Brand Issues

- Nimble, able to make changes readily
- May be an upstart in a category, having the ability to shake things up
- Less risk because of less brand equity, typically
- Low-volume manufacturing means high-unit cost per package

Big Brand Issues

- Often large, multinational corporations— therefore, move more slowly
- May be the first in a product category, having considerable market share
- High risk due to considerable brand equity
- High-volume manufacturing means low-unit cost per package

RESEARCH: Its Role within Packaging

Research is both a help and a hindrance in the design process. When presented with the right kind of insights into a brand and its consumers up front, research speeds the design process and infuses it with a deep relevance. Research used without intuition and expertise to validate a design can discourage innovation, as traditional methodologies often produce research that verifies known ideas. Designers need to understand the value and pitfalls of research and to persuade their clients to implement tools that assist design.

Build on Knowledge

The customer connection to a brand is the beginning and the ending point. It's the true impetus for design. To achieve a successful customer connection, designers must be part of the research process from the beginning.

From a communication standpoint, the design firm is usually presented with a compiled summary of all the research information—observations and data in a linear verbal format. Being removed from the research process itself leaves both the designers and the client with large interpretive gaps. The gap is, in actuality, the absence of a relationship. Successful brands are not built on knowledge

that consumers behave a certain way but rather from understanding *why* these particular consumers behave the way they do.

Studies at Retail

The most successful strategic design teams physically step into a brand's market environment to enhance their comprehension of the product or service being offered. By speaking to customers and watching them shop, design teams gain important perceptions and emotional understanding that cannot be shown on a chart or quantified in a set of data.

That process often results in designers producing breakthrough thinking for clients. The essential role of a strategic design firm that specializes in branding and packaging is to provide an identity and personality for a brand. This vital service nurtures the brand/consumer relationship by connecting clients directly with their desired customers.

Research can help meet these goals. Once in the marketplace, sitting on the crowded retail shelf, a package acts as a silent salesman. Remember, the consumer is surrounded by all kinds of salesmen graphically shouting for attention. The well-branded package speaks to its customer with the feeling and personality he or she is most comfortable with.

Create an Understanding

The right kind of research provides knowledge about what exactly is relevant to the consumer. When marketers speak with a unified voice and integrated point of view, designers get clear direction with respect to the problem at hand. Testing and acceptance studies done by focus groups don't always provide a look at the value of a design, particularly something new and exciting. It takes courage for a marketer to fly in the face of known research methods and approve bold new thinking in spite of negative findings. More and more, however, that's what it takes to surprise and delight consumers at retail.

It is not our intention to diminish the value of traditional research but rather to amplify it by adding firsthand, heart-level insight into the understanding of customer behavior. The combination ultimately benefits the brand and the bottom line.

Fresh and friendly Chicago Cutlery packaging engages and educates the consumer at the point of purchase. Laga successfully repositioned a heritage brand with its loyal following while attracting a younger affluent consumer. The brand was effectively extended through premium, mass, and accessory lines.

Packaging RESEARCH

An Interview with Cheryl Swanson, CEO, Toniq, New York, NY

Q. *What is your role at Toniq?*

A. I am a partner in and the general manager of Toniq, a strategic brand management firm. I founded the research methodologies that are at the core of our consultancy. Prior to Toniq, I worked with trend analyst, Faith Popcorn, as a marketing consultant, and then, later, went to the design side, starting the strategic practice at Wallace Church, Inc.

I realized that design firms were typically briefed by business professionals using verbal linear white papers that outlined a business problem. This didn't always make sense to creatives. Designers need symbolic and associative information to bring solutions to life. Clients needed more upstream management, and designers needed translation. At Toniq, our methods of research, which blend traditional marketing with anthropology, sociology, and psychology, improve the client/designer relationship because we figure out the territory and get the briefing in line with the business problem. Then we communicate it through visual positioning. Symbols, not words, encapsulate a brand far better. So we help move the brief away from the

subjective and eliminate antagonism caused by miscommunication of the problem designers are asked to solve.

Q. *What is the biggest challenge facing your clients?*

A. The need to understand the role of design and harness its power. Brands are all about meaning that transcends mere commercial transactions. Clients need to create products that are riveting, compelling, and instantly appealing. They need design to help achieve this. The role of design is to tell rich stories, to go beyond the decorative, enliven the senses, and captivate us all.

Q. *What role does research play in developing branding and packaging?*

A. The right research is every designer's friend. Research that is more symbolic and projective engages consumers, and they really tell you stuff. By activating consumers' imaginations, we get research that is exciting, new, and highly reflective. It tells us where a brand could go. It helps us see potential. Traditional research tells us all about the familiar. Really new concepts seem like crazy ideas and never gain

acceptance or validation through old research methods. The old protocols are definitely risk averse. In any case, research should be used as a gut check and not dictate the final decision.

Q. *In the marketing mix, what is the value of packaging?*

A. Packaging is totemic. It encapsulates the essence of the brand and lets people hold it in their hands. If branding is a story, packaging is the consumer experience of that story. For many, the package *is* the product. They are totally connected. Thus, I think package design should be more respected and valued. Advertising casts a wide net to attract and appeal, but packaging closes the deal. Design is in a transitional phase. More corporations are aware of design, but they aren't all sure what to do with it yet.

Q. *What makes a successful package design?*

A. It is an object that is intriguing and compelling. It makes people love it and pull it off a shelf. Good design reconnects us to our humanity by giving us excitement and pleasure.

Q. *What do you see as the biggest challenge for designers?*

A. Designers need to keep talking about the power of design, how it is of cultural significance; they should not just exist to support a functional, transactional purpose. Designers should also be the ambassadors of green thinking. They should address sustainability in a serious fashion for the good of the planet and all humanity. Business, with the help of designers, should solve the problem and be our salvation. It's a big challenge.

Q. *What do you see as the biggest challenge for marketers?*

A. Companies have got to transcend their concern for the bottom line.

Q. *Being a forecaster, where do you see branding and packaging going in the next five years?*

A. We need to look at a longer time horizon and take a wider view. It's up to us to embolden and push our clients. We need to encourage change and resist fear.

Case Study

Somerfield is a nationwide supermarket chain in the United Kingdom that wanted to launch a private-label pickle range. Because all pickle brands feature a photo of the product, designers at Taxi Studio used one as well, but with a twist.

What MBAs Know About
RESEARCH and DESIGN

An Interview with Bobby J. Calder, *Kellogg School of Business, Northwestern University, Chicago, IL*

Q. *What is your role at the Kellogg School of Management?*

A. I am a professor of marketing in the Marketing Department at the Kellogg School of Business, Northwestern University. I also teach a class in consumer psychology in the journalism program at Northwestern.

Q. *How do you prepare your students to work with designers?*

A. I think it is a challenge for all MBA programs to get students prepared to work in cross-disciplinary teams with a variety of experts, like designers. There is a problem in getting MBAs to understand what design can bring to the party, but there is also a difficulty in getting designers to understand business problems.

Q. *What can art schools do in preparing their students to work with MBAs?*

A. Design is a process, but at the heart of it is art, even in a professional context. That spurs creativity, but it also fosters the idea that design is sacrosanct. The leading way to get off track is to have a design that its creator views as art and not as the solution to a business problem.

Q. *How do you view branding in its relationship to packaging?*

A. I don't really like the word "packaging." I think it trivializes what designers do. I like "brand design" as a description. Brand is an idea that you're trying to create in consumers' minds. It's not just a communications activity, the product must deliver on the idea as well. Packaging is one of the most important ways of expressing a brand. You take an abstract idea and concretize it. Brand design brings the brand idea to life.

Q. *What do you see as the biggest challenge for marketers?*

A. More and more companies are recognizing design as important. The danger is that since companies are always looking for a "magic bullet" to solve all their problems, they may see design in that role. But the truth is, design is not a magic bullet. It's an important part of a mix of things.

Q. *What do you think of the research on package design?*

A. I don't like the way designs are tested. I hate to bring design into focus groups. You're asking people to become "design experts," and it is very difficult for them to articulate their perceptions. I like research methods that expose people to designs very quickly then ask for three or four adjectives to describe their impression. Consumers are not meant to think about package design, they are meant to experience it.

Q. *Where do you see brand design going in the next five years?*

A. My hope is that more companies will see brand design as a fundamental. It's the only way to fight parity. Everyone in marketing sees branding as important. You can't have a great brand without great brand design.

Case Study

Partida Tequila successfully launched in June of 2005 in five states on par with sales of the premium vodka brands today, by focusing on Partida Tequila's inherent attributes, Bright Design captured the essence of the brand, as well as true tequila culture.

How Consumers Absorb **INFORMATION**

The research that is most useful in informing the package design process indicates what consumers think and feel about a brand.

Targeting Consumers

Most consumer insights are gained through a combination of sociology, psychology, anthropology, economics, and statistics. Targeting audiences is done using a variety of segmentation concepts. Information is observed as *demographics*, which are the quantifiable characteristics of consumers (that is, who, what, where, when, and why, expressed in numbers), and *psychographics*, which studies behavioral variables that indicate why people do

what they do (personality type, buying patterns, goals and aspirations, special interests, and lifestyle choices).

For any brand packaging to work, it must be tailored to the audience that will receive it. Defining a target audience is a means of striking a balance between mass marketing and customized individual messaging.

Consumer Decision Making

The target consumer may change from brand to brand, product to product. What never changes are the stages of a consumer's decision-making process. A review of this process shows a variety of opportunities for design to propel a consumer toward buying a product.

Studies show that there are typically five stages of consumer behavior:

1. Problem recognition:
The consumer perceives a need, which triggers the idea of making a purchase. This can be activated by marketing and advertising messages.

2. Information search:
The consumer seeks value and looks at options for meeting the need. Past experience, brand affinity, referrals from friends and authorities, and sales people are considered.

Case Study

Ciao Bella gelatos and sorbets packaging, designed by Wallace Church, features an elegant simplicity to create striking high-impact shelf appeal. The graphics for this premium Italian frozen treat helped garner the brand $15 million (£5 million) in sales in 2007.

3. Evaluation of alternatives:
The consumer assesses value by analyzing the gathered information. Personal criteria and emotional and rational factors are at play.

4. Purchase decision:
The consumer decides to buy the product based on perceived value. He chooses the place to buy it based on price, availability, terms of sale, retail location, or past experience. He also must choose when to buy it. Alternatively, he simply decides not to buy.

5. Post-purchase behavior:
The consumer finds value in consuming or using the product, or the product does not address the original need.

Measuring a
DESIGN'S EFFECTIVENESS

Designers have a limited amount of space on each package, and they need to maximize every inch. Perception Research Services (PRS) has developed PRS Eye-Tracking as a method for measuring a design system's ability to gain and hold attention. According to PRS, "Our research has found that people typically spend under ten seconds at most grocery categories and typically fail to even see and consider over 33 percent of the brands in each category. For a design system to be effective, it must break through clutter and hold attention long enough to implant a message."

Using in-store scenarios and hidden cameras, the researchers gauge consumers' behavior at the shelf, how long their eyes scan, and exactly where on the package their eyes focus. These studies determine the relationship between design elements and their effect.

One point to remember is that consumers may spend a lot of time looking at a package because it is either wonderfully compelling or totally confusing. Thus, any research of this nature should document how consumers behave and then look deeper through follow-up interviews to uncover why they acted as they did.

Case Study

Optima Soulsight reinvigorated a premier choco-
latier with a bold new package, whimsical illustration, and a renewed connection with its foodie
core consumer. Sales from the all-occasion line
grew 35 percent in the first year of the redesign.

Brand ESSENCE/Brand POSITIONING

Why do consumers buy one brand over another? Rational thought does play into purchase intent. Factors such as price and perceived product quality are two rational concerns, for example. However, when everything is the same and products appear at parity, consumers' decisions often become emotional.

Left, Right, and Branded

For many years, there has been talk of the left and right sides of the human brain. The left side controls the rational, analytical, and scientific, while the right works on the emotional and artistic.

Great package designers blend both science and art in their work. One area where this comes into play is branding. Designers must create and then present their work in the context of branding terms in order to sell their ideas effectively to clients. Often these terms are confusing or seemingly similar, but it is essential to understand how they relate to each and every packaging project.

Brand Promise

The first thing to consider is the brand promise—that is, the one thing the brand intends to own in the target consumer's mind. Brand promises must be believable, clear, unique, compelling, and endearing to the consumer. All marketing and communication tools must reinforce the promise such that the brand is shown to be uniquely qualified to deliver on it.

Brand Values

At the core of any brand's identity are brand values—the things the company believes in. Brand values guide all decisions and provide a framework for corporate culture, marketing communications, and the brand's public personality.

Brand Essence

From there, consider brand essence, the intrinsic properties that characterize or identify the brand—its heart and soul. Brand essence is concise, enduring, aspirational yet attainable, and extendable. It is a distillation of the brand's identity and an encapsulation of a brand's values. It is not a tagline or logo; rather, it is the rich, multidimensional character of a brand, and it must be conveyed in every aspect of the consumer's experience with a product.

Brand Positioning

Related to brand promise, and informed by brand essence, brand positioning is the place a brand adopts in its competitive environment to ensure that consumers see it. Positioning sets a brand apart and connects consumers to products. With brand positioning, the entire marketing mix is carefully manipulated in order to communicate, teach, and inform consumers that this is the best product for them. Done properly, positioning can turn customers into brand evangelists.

All of these aspects of branding are tools to shape design. The goals of creating integrated harmony and strong impressions in the minds of consumers should be the designer's guiding principles in packaging.

The **CHANGING ROLE** of Packaging

An Interview with Daniel Hachard, *Nestlé Zone Champion, Generating Demand Lead for Zone America, Los Angeles, CA*

Q. *How do you view branding in its relationship to packaging?*

A. For me, and for consumers, the brand is the point of reference when choosing a product. It's the difference between taking a risk or not with a product. It's about trust. On a package, it's of paramount importance.

Q. *In the marketing mix, what is the value of packaging?*

A. Packaging is the most important and least expensive. It is the commercial vehicle that lasts longest and has the most impact. Packaging has stopping power at the retail shelf. You get the most bang for your money with packaging.

Q. *What makes a successful package design?*

A. Packaging must be seen as a holistic proposition. It must fulfill both the emotional and physical expectations of consumers. It must connect with consumers on both levels. A successful package provides benefits to the consumer. For example, it can be a functional benefit—it's easy to hold, dispense, and dispose of. On an emotional level, packaging creates trust in a brand. It allows consu-

mers to react to emotional cues such as wellness, nutrition, or appetite appeal.

In the end, there are four ways to make a package successful:

1. Make it simple in the way you speak to consumers.
2. Increase visual impact through branding, photography, and graphics.
3. Reinforce the brand and let its essence come through. Show the DNA of the brand.
4. Be innovative and creative.

Q. *What do you see as the biggest challenge for designers?*

A. The biggest challenges for designers are staying ahead of technology and being creative. They need to be courageous about design. They need to develop packaging that looks irresistible to consumers. Designers must work to be relevant. They need to be flexible in the face of corporate changes, acquisitions, or budget constraints. When a company is under pressure, they will put all their vendors under pressure. This can mean designers adjusting their processes for faster turnaround times. Products are going to market faster.

We as clients need to keep designers informed. When they understand the problem fully, they can be more helpful.

Q. *What brands/packages do you admire, and why?*

A. I admire Lexus, Apple, Starbucks, and Nespresso. All are incredible brands. All stand for uncompromising quality, service, and innovation. They really understand their brand essence and live it and breathe it.

Q. *If you could change one thing within the branding and packaging industry, what would it be?*

A. A change in consciousness is needed. The United States needs to develop a deeper and more genuine concern for the environment. Packaging has a huge environmental impact. In Europe, designers and manufacturers have it in mind, think about it more, and are more concerned about it. But, in the states, consumers are more concerned about it. Global warming is a deep concern to us all.

Q. *What is the single biggest mistake you see in the package design process?*

A. Design briefs that are not good enough. Either they are wrong or have incomplete information. Sometimes we overcomplicate everything. We are all consumers, pretty much driven by basic needs. Sure we have to have methodologies and research, but sometimes, as a result, we over intellectualize. Things should be more simple.

Q. *Where do you see this industry going in the next five years?*

A. The packaging industry and packages themselves will change. We'll see more intelligent packages—they will talk to you. Packages will calculate the right nutritional value. There will be more multilingual packages.

I think the design industry is in a good place. The power of design in packaging has yet to be fully recognized. People are beginning to talk about it. If brands really want to be successful, they've got to use creativity and innovation as an edge. We see more design revitalization projects happening on shorter cycles.

These three Nestlé brands, Good Start by CBX, Coffeemate by Cornerstone Strategic Branding, Inc., and Treasures by Thompson Design Group, demonstrate that packaging is much more than just a simple container for a given product.

THE PACKAGING TREND CYCLE

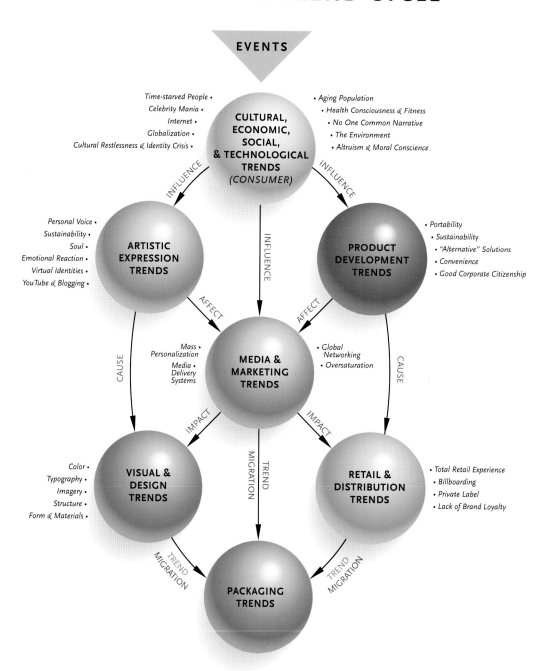

EVENTS

Time-starved People •
Celebrity Mania •
Internet •
Globalization •
Cultural Restlessness & Identity Crisis •

CULTURAL, ECONOMIC, SOCIAL, & TECHNOLOGICAL TRENDS (CONSUMER)

• Aging Population
• Health Consciousness & Fitness
• No One Common Narrative
• The Environment
• Altruism & Moral Conscience

INFLUENCE

Personal Voice •
Sustainability •
Soul •
Emotional Reaction •
Virtual Identities •
YouTube & Blogging •

ARTISTIC EXPRESSION TRENDS

PRODUCT DEVELOPMENT TRENDS

• Portability
• Sustainability
• "Alternative" Solutions
• Convenience
• Good Corporate Citizenship

AFFECT

Mass •
Personalization
Media •
Delivery
Systems

MEDIA & MARKETING TRENDS

• Global Networking
• Oversaturation

CAUSE

Color •
Typography •
Imagery •
Structure •
Form & Materials •

VISUAL & DESIGN TRENDS

RETAIL & DISTRIBUTION TRENDS

• Total Retail Experience
• Billboarding
• Private Label
• Lack of Brand Loyalty

IMPACT

TREND MIGRATION

PACKAGING TRENDS

TREND MIGRATION

Packaging trends are influenced by a larger set of strategic issues that grow out of a variety of consumer, artistic, business, and media trends. Understanding trends helps designers entertain, influence, inform, and motivate consumers' product purchase decisions.

Packaging **TRENDS**

Throughout history, trends have affected and shaped society and defined human progress. They mirror our attitudes, values, desires, and dreams. We live in a multidimensional world where fads and trends overlap and collide, all vying for our attention as they speed around the globe via the Internet. We have learned to filter out much of this information, absorbing only what we see as relevant. To help deal with mass-market clutter, our society fragments itself into subcultures. Through these groups, we can observe a trend incubate and grow from idiosyncratic idea into mass appeal.

How Trends Work

A trend's life cycle looks a lot like a bell curve. Typically, it gains momentum as increasing numbers of people adopt it, but once it reaches mass appeal, interest declines or stabilizes as the trend moves into the mainstream, or else it simply dies out as another trend catches on and begins to grow. The process by which a new trend, idea, or product is accepted in the marketplace is called *diffusion*. Theories abound on the mechanics of diffusion, including the Everett Rogers Diffusion of Innovations Theory, which is widely accepted.

How Trends Work in Packaging

Because packaging is so closely linked to consumer preferences, it is here that trends are transformed into functional applications; packages help sell products. However, package design is also where the adoption of a trend can get complicated. If you are too early, you can miss your target consumer; too late, and you are seen as old news. Thus visual concepts that express trends must be applied with careful consideration of the product's brand and its promise. Does the trend actually fit the brand, and will it attract the right buyer?

In packaging, trends tend to grow slowly because longer lead times are required to make changes. We see early adopters and influencers coming from small start-up brands, which have less at risk, while it may take years before big brands catch on to a trend. When we see large brands begin to use a trend, we know this trend is reaching the top of the bell curve.

Within the marketplace, it can be challenging to pick out new and emerging trends, as there are many different stages of a trend's life cycle. Also, consumers are at different stages of acceptance within the bell curve of a trend, so it's vital to understand the products' consumer. You must learn the buying habits of specific target audiences in order to better understand their comfort zone and how far the packaging can stretch and motivate them to purchase. It's about knowing how far the brand you are designing for can be pushed.

How Designers Work with Trends

It is vital for designers to understand what motivates and establishes visual trends. For the most part, these concepts are directly influenced by the environment, societal attitudes, and beliefs.

In spotting and evaluating packaging trends, we have to keep in mind that designers are working with a consistent palette of tools that can be viewed as trendsetting in themselves. This palette includes color, typography, imagery, structure, form, and materials. Any one of these design elements can be used to express a trend.

INNOVATION Born from Art and Science

How Innovation Is a Function of Art and Science

Innovation is the buzzword of the new millennium. While globalization and the pursuit of revenue are the driving forces behind most innovation, in an era of constant change, maximizing the possibilities and finding the niche that can redefine a category or spark a sales revolution is always top of mind. That is a goal both left brain and right brain thinkers share.

How can these two very different yet similar groups—designers and their clients—collaborate to create packaging that cuts through the clutter?

Here are a few ways to develop a relationship that results in innovation:

- **Encourage collaboration**. Fundamental to any successful creative endeavor is the synergy of the team involved.

- **Stress communication**. Understand how different team members process information.

- **Remain openminded**. Acknowledging other people's disciplines and stresses allows you to judge and comment on project issues more objectively.

- **Nurture everyone's strengths**. Encourage and allow other people to share the spotlight and show their talents.

- **Clarify and share your vision**. Make certain every team member has the same goals.

- **Embrace complexity and uncertainty**. Enjoy the challenge by accepting the unknown.

- **Respect the courage it takes to make bold decisions**. Is the team climbing Mount Everest or just going to the top of the building? Does the team have consensus? No guts, no glory.

Expanding Your Creativity

Creativity is the ability to produce work that is both novel and appropriate. Innovation is the result of creative thinking. Toward that end, an expansion of creativity shakes up the old and opens up new ideas. Try these approaches:

- Practice making unusual and unexpected mental associations
- Rearrange and alter the balance of attributes
- Acquire information in many areas
- Develop good skills so you can concentrate on being creative rather than focused on mastering one plan
- Work hard. Creativity is not the product but the process
- Be confident
- Be persistent
- Be perceptive
- Be prepared for criticism
- Seek help in your weaker areas
- Focus on what you love to do

Case Study

Feldmann + Schultchen Design Studios GmbH created the packaging for fish marketers, Deutsche See, to appeal to sophisticated shoppers as the ultimate in freshness. The unusual nesting structure and materials convey premium status and appetite appeal, and the package functions well for stacking and display at retail. Innovations such as the packaging's, volume reduction, and the universal conveyer belt capability of the packages have been patented.

The **wow** Factor

A wow product is one that has defined and draws attention to a new or existing category. Its brand or package is a direct reflection of the product attributes. Wow products make us stop and take notice. Consumers want to have relationships with them. Wow makes connections bigger than mere product loyalty. When consumers think of these products, they think of nothing else. Wow blows away the competition.

Defining WOW

DuPuis is always on the lookout for wow. We spent time thinking about what would qualify for wow and how would we identify wow packages. We developed this definition of wow:

- It elevates perception within the category.
- It creates interest and involves the consumer on different levels.
- It is groundbreaking in its approach.
- The brand and product feel at one with each other.
- It stands out in a sea of sameness.
- It emotionally touches its audience.

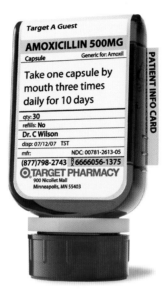

The Target ClearRx prescription bottle was designed by Deborah Adler. Here function, system, and form are perfected. The package makes the prescription easy to use and decreases the likelihood of a consumer taking the wrong medicine—an excellent example of how design can and does solve problems—without sacrificing aesthetics. Here the solution is one that is clear and simple fulfilling a need through a very creative solution.

Pom Wonderful, designed by their internal design team. Pom Wonderful started the pomegranate juice trend, and its bold, memorable bottle quickly grew to stand for health. Here we see the power of owning a unique shape. It not only defines its category; it stands out from everything else. The shape and the name create allure and appeal for a largely unknown product.

A private label can be a brand unto itself. This is what Target has achieved with Archer Farms, developed by MOD and the Target in-house design team. Its design captivates through unique packaging structures, engaging photography, and elements of nostalgia, delivering a premium quality perception and demonstrating that a store brand can rise above the generic stereotype. The brand identity is prominent, but not large—it is an understated approach that places emphasis on the food.

Not Guilty was developed by designers VBAT for Freeez light ice cream treats as an entirely new and distinctive brand concept. As a theme, and as proof that there's nothing wrong with enjoying tasty things, the Not Guilty packages are brought to life by a number of situations where actors are photographed "caught in the act"—unable to resist temptation. The cheeky humor has proven irresistible to consumers and sales have doubled since the new packaging was implemented.

UNLOCKING THE
POWER OF DESIGN

Six keys to success

[1] Don't React—**PROACT**

[2] Connect on an **EMOTIONAL LEVEL**

[3] Don't Settle for **PARITY**

[4] Focus on **CORE VALUES**

[5] **VALIDATE** Appropriately

[6] **COLLABORATE**

The Six Keys to **SUCCESS**

The keys to success described here were developed by reviewing numerous packaging design programs, both triumphs and failures. We know success can be measured many ways, so we looked at what drove project effectiveness in terms of both sales and aesthetic accomplishment. All too often, designers and their clients use different criteria to evaluate packaging solutions. To us, that doesn't make sense—all participants in the creative process should focus on both the art and the science of packaging to create breakthrough design.

Success Dynamics

At DuPuis, we typically present these keys to success as general points to take into consideration during the preliminary assessment of a packaging project. Not addressing them early and often are major impediments to success. We observe that when even just one of them is not implemented, results suffer. However, these keys are by no means the only drivers to success. The dynamics of any packaging program include team interactions, product offering, subjective interpretation, distribution channels, budget constraints, and manufacturing capabilities, all of which can and do affect results.

Team Success

Great packaging finds its origins in a strong and talented team. When we say team, we are referring to both the design professionals involved in the process and the client. The assumption is that these two groups will collaborate on the project. Talent and ideas will flow from both sides. Open-mindedness and mutual respect from both groups is mandatory. Teams must ask these questions as they embark on the process: Are we working well together? Are we capable of working well together? Do we mutually respect each other's disciplines? Are our goals aligned? Positive answers to these questions are vital to success. It's why clients so often work with agencies and designers they know and with whom they are friendly. Often, success is not simply measured by the end product but also by the experience along the way. As a designer, this is your brand experience, and, in addition to your creative skill, it's what you're selling. Service, experience, and talent are a given in this industry. They are the ultimate keys to success.

Package design that strikes a meaningful chord with the consumer and drives increased purchase intent is great marketing. It requires close collaboration between designers and clients. Success can not happen without trust. These six keys to success help stack the deck in favor of achieving greater results for both marketers and designers.

[1] Don't React—**PROACT**

In the world of consumer packaged goods, the competition is fierce and the search for innovative ways to differentiate is a constant endeavor. Many look to innovate their products by offering new and improved versions, while others use creative advertising campaigns and engaging promotions. Increasingly, more are turning to branding and packaging revitalizations.

Staying Ahead

Timing is critical in keeping on top of changing ideas and influences on consumer preference. Brands that don't keep pace with the times can quickly see their market share erode. Often packaging is the last arena to be viewed as an area for improvement. We say "Don't react—proact" because we see that successful companies value the affect packaging can have on the purchase behavior. And in doing so, these are the companies that take a proactive approach to branding and packaging—they lead the market, not follow it.

Market Conditions

Each product industry has its own market conditions, development time, growth season, and distribution channels. Keeping up with all this information, along with constantly looking at their brand's relevance to consumers, is a big challenge for marketers. Designers need to understand how these conditions affect package design considerations and assist their clients by keeping them informed of visual trends that support marketers' goals.

Brand Equity

It's essential to be true to the brand when evaluating trends and market shifts. Don't do change for its own sake. Change must make strategic sense. Consumers want and crave creative ideas—but in keeping with the brand's personality.

Established brands have equities that represent and stand for attributes of the brand's promise. These are key visual elements, and some can and some cannot be altered. Deciding what is equity is typically dependent on consumer insights.

Many companies have realized the power of being proactive instead of reacting to market conditions. These brands tend to update their visual presentation before it becomes tired, keeping consumes surprised. The children's shampoo, left, by Turner Duckworth; the frozen entrée packaging by Wallace Church, top right; and the canned vegetables by Philippe Becker Design, all took a proactive stance.

Case Study | Dole Organics

Built from a firm belief in fair trade practices and sustainable farming methods such as soil rejuvenation, crop rotation and natural methods of pest control, Dole sought to launch an organic line of nutritious frozen fruit, Dole Organics. As a leader in both fresh and packaged produce, Dole knows that fruit should be allowed to ripen in the field where it reaches its maximum flavor. It's exactly at that point that it's frozen to lock in all its natural goodness. Because the quality of the product lives up to such expectations, the packaging needed to communicate a feeling of natural abundance and from-the-source wholesomeness. The spirited emphasis of the design is the product, its fresh origin, and the care taken to produce it. That focus not only allows the package to communicate that it is organic, but more importantly, the practical and emotional reasons why organic makes a difference. Dole Organics, designed by DuPuis, makes a positive and bold statement among neighboring brands that wellness, nutrition, and social responsibility matter.

[2] Connect on an **EMOTIONAL LEVEL**

When consumers shop, they walk the aisles of a store looking for just the right product. They may go to a particular section searching for anything in that category, or they may look for a specific brand, or they may be drawn there by a special promotion. When they do find what they are looking for, consumers are faced with several brand offerings of the same type of product. It is here that packaging must do its work of selling.

Consumer Selection

For retail success, designers and marketers must know what motivates a purchase in the category. Price is a factor and always has been, but what if your product is higher priced? In this case, your buyer must be drawn to your package—not just from an impact standpoint but with the emotional conviction that it is worth the extra money. With consumers spending mere seconds to make a selection in most categories, visual elements must work effectively and efficiently. This is done through the designer's palette of structure, photography, typography, illustration, and graphic elements. With this combined aesthetic approach, packaging creates a sensory experience. Sensory perceptions, properly directed and positioned, relate directly to concepts of value, price, and quality. Consumers obtain a deeper reason to believe, one that can make them feel justified in paying more for a product.

Elicit Response

An emotional connection between a consumer and a brand is the result of the brand's consistent expression and concise implementation throughout all media touchpoints, culminating when the consumer is face to face with the product on the shelf. There the package must live up to the already formed brand impression. Furthermore, it must convey that the product is beyond its competitors. If the product is exactly the same as others, then the package must work to romance and seduce the buyer. This is the emotional element.

From beverages like Pearlfisher's water, Michael Nash's chocolate drink, and a special edition Coca-Cola by A Designer's Republic, to olive oil by Waitrose (provided by Consume UK), packaging can surprise, amuse, and draw consumers into a relationship with the product.

A growing body of consumer-behavior research shows that people may rationalize buying decisions based on a set of facts, but they purchase based on feelings. Buying isn't necessarily a rational decision; it's often an emotional one.

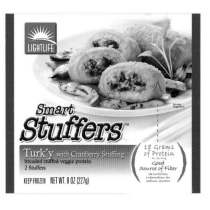

Case Study | Lightlife

With the rising interest in healthy meat alternatives, meatless products such as Lightlife are now positioning themselves to appeal to broader audiences. To succeed in the general marketplace, healthy vegetarian brands are speaking more definitively to skeptical mainstream consumers concerned about taste.

To convince consumers of Lightlife's great flavor and health benefits, DuPuis focused on presenting the food in a relevant and inviting arrangement. The Smart Stuffers and other Lightlife vegetarian meat substitutes are placed on an array of fresh vegetables atop a clean, simple, white plate. The photography ignites an emotional response and works to convince the senses that this is delicious food. The package involves the consumer while communicating key benefits in a casual manner commensurate with the brand's lighthearted healthy personality.

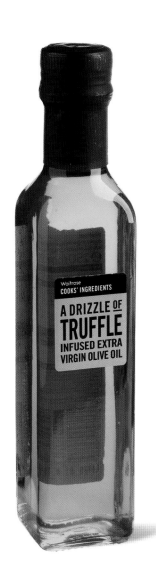

[3] Don't Settle for **PARITY**

Many packages are overlooked on the shelf; in fact, according to Perception Research Services, Inc. (PRS), over 30 percent are not even seen by consumers. Achieving shelf impact doesn't mean just shouting louder than the products next to you, it means understanding what will draw your consumer to your package. The target consumer may be lured by packages featuring clean simplicity, a photographic style, certain shapes and colors, or certain kinds of typography. Whatever the design specifics, a package must become the only one a target buyer sees.

Designing Differentiation
Unfortunately, too often, consumers find lots of similar-looking packages that form a sea of sameness. There is parity, or seemingly equal value, in packaging and products. Many companies start out with good intentions but get bogged down by their own internal processes. Marketing teams become fearful of too big of a change, concerned it could result in loss of revenue. With corporations' margins so tight, this is an understandable concern. Designers must lead clients to effective solutions that speak to their concerns in a creative way. This is what can make packaging design more difficult than many other design disciplines: It is highly strategic, and success is tied to sales.

Parity Line
Designers and marketers need to observe a product's position in relationship to its competition by determining where it falls on the parity line. Is the brand taking risks and standing out by being above the line? Or is it playing it safe, blending in with competitors, and staying below the line?

Calculated Risks
Taking a design above the parity line requires clients to be courageous and designers to use their intuition about what will create breakthrough. Typical research methodologies do not necessarily work well in quantifying the new and different. Focus groups rarely accept something new and different, hence breakthrough concepts are left behind and parity is accepted.

Designers shouldn't become frustrated by clients' fear of change and reluctance to take risks. Fighting parity is worth being uncomfortable.

Great brands stand out. Plum baby food by Brand Engine, Sonnentor teas by d.signwerk, Method furniture cleaner by Karim Rashid, and Homebase BBQ equipment by Turner Duckworth all live above the parity line and get noticed at retail.

Case Study | Munchkin

For mothers looking for products for their children, it is vital that brands and packages not only be visible in the store environment but also speak to these buyers' rational and emotional senses. Munchkin's mission is to rid the world of tired and mundane products by developing clever, innovative ones that excite and delight both parents and their children.

At first, Munchkin requested the product be placed in a traditional box. The DuPuis creative team pushed them to move the product outside the box and showcase these toys' unique qualities. Doing this allowed for strong shelf presence and enhanced consumer involvement by allowing them to engage in each toys' learning benefits.

The new packaging structure was groundbreaking for products within the toy category. It has since been copied and adopted by competitors, which is why great brands must constantly be looking for what's next.

[4] Focus on **CORE VALUES**

Core values are the beliefs and ideas an organization holds dear. They are part of the DNA of an organization and are often inspired by the views of the founders. When explicitly stated, core values become an oral or written expression of a company's brand and corporate culture.

While strategies and tactics may change, core values always remain the same. Therefore, it is imperative to remain focused on these values when crafting marketing strategies, managing brands, and positioning products. Many companies use core values to set performance standards and direct the implementation of their mission in everything from product offerings to package design.

Show Respect

Every product created, marketed, and sold should reflect the core values of the company. In addition, every package should adhere to the Fair Packaging and Labeling Act and other governmental standards and regulations, such as the U.S. Food and Drug Administration (FDA). Packages thus uphold the truth and respect the integrity of the company as well as the government.

Core values should not be confused with slogans or mottos, which are marketing tools that often bear little relation to the actual philosophy of an organization.

Integrity, Innovation, and Ingenuity

In an image-saturated environment where practically anything can act as a surface for promoting a product, staying focused on core values can help guide the creative process and support the development of a package that represents the people who created the product. If succinct and authentic, core values can help brand managers, art directors, and other creative professionals make correct decisions.

At the end of the day, values define who a company is and what it stands for. They explain in simple language why it's in business and express the mindset and behaviors its leaders believe will lead to success. As a designer, when you stay focused on the client's values you are more likely to achieve the client's objective quickly and efficiently and help build a strong brand.

Looking after brand DNA is an essential part of package design. Core values provide a roadmap for success. They are part of expressing a brand's distinctive qualities to the consumer through the packaging.

Wallace Church's Heinz Cocktail Sauces, Zunda Group's various Newman's Own products, and Pearlfisher's Absolut 100 vodka all express each brand's unique DNA.

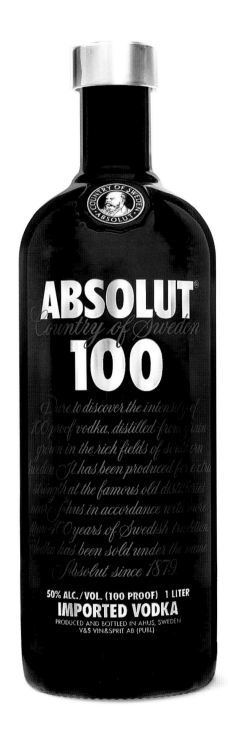

Case Study | Country Crock

Staying true to core values is challenging when migrating a brand into a new category. Many opportunities to expand product lines present themselves, but are they right for the brand? For Country Crock the opportunity to bring the brand into the prepared side dishes category proved to be a successful venture that also elevated the perception of its original spreads business.

The goal was to capture existing as well as new consumers with the new product offerings. However, the brand team felt that Country Crock Side Dishes might have a different target consumer than the spreads business does. Considerations were made to interpret the brand, keeping true to its core values, while developing a design architecture that also spoke to new audiences. DuPuis worked with key brand equities, using farm fresh imagery and established equity colors to create a brand foundation.

Country Crock Side Dishes grew rapidly, becoming over a 100 million dollar (£51 million) business in a short time.

[5] **VALIDATE** Appropriately

Before

After

If consumer research were an exact science, new products would not have a failure rate over 90 percent. Research has its place within the development of packaging, but it can't be the only tool for validation. What type of research is conducted, and for what purpose, is important to address. Buying behaviors and opinions about products change from what is said in focus groups to what actually happens in a retail arena. Sometimes quick, off-the-cuff impressions are much more valuable than results gleaned from exhaustive interviews.

Judging Research

Psychology plays an important role in buying habits. Also, consumer behavior changes depending on age, gender, culture, and economic status. Each client has its own opinions on the subject of research, with some companies mandating research findings as the final judge in evaluating packaging design. Research is often viewed as the only science in the package development process, so it is seen as truth.

There is a risk involved with taking research too literally. We would not have many of the cool products and packages we see today if research findings were the only factors considered. Just because a design is popular (or not) in limited consumer tests doesn't mean it's actually going to be the most effective one in the marketplace. Research often tells you where you have been, but it doesn't tell you where you are going. It's like trying to give directions while constantly looking in the rearview mirror.

Simulating Purchase

We believe the most useful research approach for validating package design is to simulate the introduction of a new product by observing consumers at the shelf. Placing a new packaging concept in a retail context gives a realistic sense of its impact. Getting great consumer feedback in point-of-sale research can be time-consuming and expensive, but it is an important tool for success.

Case Study | Ro*Tel

Revitalizing a well-established, iconic brand is challenging. What is the brand story consumers are connecting with? How can the revitalized brand enhance the emotional experience? The right research can be insightful and complementary in forging meaningful connections. Research can give designers the background and knowledge to develop a more concise solution that will actually enhance the brand.

Brand strategy consultants at Toniq provided initial research that gave the design team at DuPuis key information for a successful redesign of the Ro*Tel brand products. This included visual interpretations of the brand image. It was a key factor in creating designs in line with Ro*Tel's deep roots in delivering food packed with fresh southwestern flavor.

[6] COLLABORATE

Packaging design is not a solitary endeavor. It requires the expertise of many professionals. Whether the client is the owner, president, marketing director, or packaging manager, he or she brings valuable insights and knowledge that is essential for packaging to succeed.

Design is a journey of discovery, and solutions can be found by taking a variety of paths. Creative meetings, even brainstorming sessions, with your client can be exceptionally valuable.

Include Clients

Contrary to the old-school design development process, which kept clients at bay by showing them a formal presentation only after weeks of isolated creative development, we find a more open collaboration from the start allows for easier client acceptance of a design. This allows relationships to form, leading to mutual trust and understanding of each other's talents. Furthermore, a deeper knowledge of the product is developed.

Work Together

Successful collaboration requires defining the working relationship. Who is leading? How will decisions be made? No matter how you look at it, the client has the final say. It is our job as designers to develop others' trust in and respect for our profession. Our solutions must be in alignment with clients' goals and objectives, not our personal aesthetic preferences. Design solutions must be communicated with business in mind and spoken about from a marketer's point of view.

Creative Journey

Design is powerful and effective. However, clients often don't realize how valuable it can be to their bottom line. Few companies today use design to its fullest potential. When clients understand the benefits of design, great collaboration can make their creative journeys more effective.

When clients look to find the cheapest solution without valuing design, the collaboration is likely to fail. The resulting packages are rarely new and typically lack passion and emotional direction. In the end, ineffective collaboration takes a product to the same place as its competitors, joining the world of sameness.

Case Study | Sam's Choice

Store brands, also known as private-label products, have risen in quality and perceived value in the last decade to become established brands rivaling their big-brand competitors. Design is a real factor in the increased market share of private label.

For Wal-Mart, the redesign of a successful flavored water line, Sam's Choice Clear American, needed to keep its value positioning but leverage design to spur further interest and attract new consumers. The experience for Braue-DuPuis' creative team working with Wal-Mart to revitalize the water was collaborative and respectful, even though only one face-to-face meeting took place.

Technology allowed for smooth-running team relationships to develop through telephone and email communications. The collaborative nature of the team allowed for open dialog, giving the designers the freedom and flexibility to develop targeted creative that hit the mark.

THE PACKAGING
PROCESS

Navigating a package design from concept to completion

THE PACKAGING PROCESS
—12-week sample model—

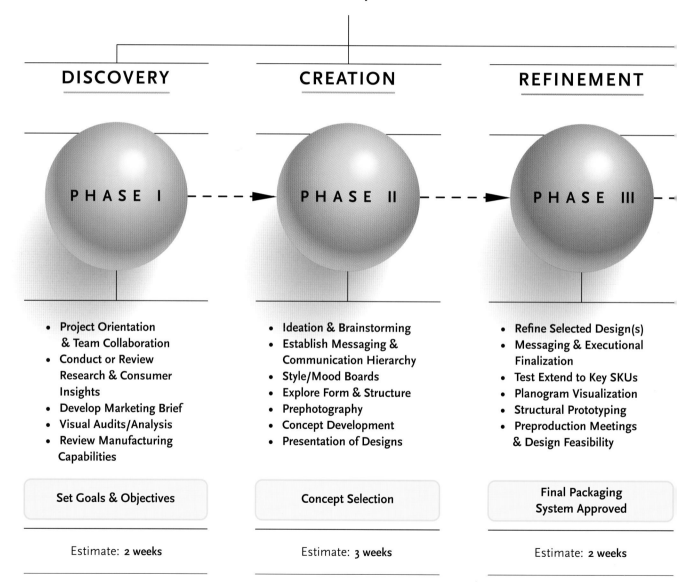

DISCOVERY

PHASE I

- Project Orientation & Team Collaboration
- Conduct or Review Research & Consumer Insights
- Develop Marketing Brief
- Visual Audits/Analysis
- Review Manufacturing Capabilities

Set Goals & Objectives

Estimate: **2 weeks**

CREATION

PHASE II

- Ideation & Brainstorming
- Establish Messaging & Communication Hierarchy
- Style/Mood Boards
- Explore Form & Structure
- Prephotography
- Concept Development
- Presentation of Designs

Concept Selection

Estimate: **3 weeks**

REFINEMENT

PHASE III

- Refine Selected Design(s)
- Messaging & Executional Finalization
- Test Extend to Key SKUs
- Planogram Visualization
- Structural Prototyping
- Preproduction Meetings & Design Feasibility

Final Packaging System Approved

Estimate: **2 weeks**

IMPLEMENTATION

PHASE IV

- Complete Photography
- Planogram Finalization
- Finalize Design for All Package Surfaces
- Line Extensions Complete
- Dieline Verification/ Complete Structural 3-D Rendering

Content & Design
Approval for all SKUs

Estimate: **3 weeks**

PRODUCTION

PHASE V

- High-Resolution File Preparation to Spec
- Color Correction
- Press Check/Printing
- Create Standards and/or Packaging Style Guides
- Archiving Asset Management

Release of Final Art
& Print Management

Estimate: **2 weeks**

This diagram shows a simplified overview of the steps by which a package goes from concept to completion. This process serves as a model but can be modified to suit each project. The factors that affect the flow and order of the steps are:

- *General scope of the packaging program.* For example, massive packaging programs (tens or even hundreds of SKUs) often consist of waves of implementation and production to match forecasted shelf dates, whereas a one- or two-SKU project may skip implementation. Also, a simple line extension initiative or package refresh might bypass many steps and even phases.

- *Research needs and available data at program onset.* Existing research may be suitable from the start and not require new testing initiatives in discovery. Conversely, a new product or a brand breaking into a new category may require extensive positioning or psychographic research in discovery and one or more rounds of validation research during creation, refinement, and even implementation. Also, messaging is sometimes known at a program onset, but it often is developed during creation and refinement.

- *Timing constraints.* When time is short, a truncated version of this model is necessary. The first steps to go are usually in the discovery and refinement phases. When time and budget are abundant, the process can take its full course and even cycle back.

Phase 1: Gathering **KNOWLEDGE**

The more all members of the packaging team collaborate and pool their various disciplinary perspectives right from the beginning of the discovery phase, the more successful the outcome will be. Of course, the process must be time-managed properly, and the person who makes the final decision must be clearly identified as well.

The Right Research

Research and consumer testing take several common forms: brand DNA or essence testing, quantitative and qualitative interviewing, focus groups, commercial eye-tracking, in-home user tests (IHUTs), and so on. Choosing among them is a mixed methodology beginning with the identification of what knowledge is sought. Once this is identified, appropriate research formats can be chosen, but time and budgetary limitations are almost always big factors.

The key to getting the most out of research is balance; research must be used in conjunction with intuition and instinct.

Today's business climate often inadvertently discourages placing much weight on instinct and gut feelings because Wall Street wants proof, not hypothesis. The typical corporate environment is understandably risk-adverse. Unfortunately, this culture means product parity and me-too positioning. Data and findings compiled during research are vital to measuring buying habits, opinions, and needs, but do not give birth to breakaway ideas. Properly interpreted, research can either validate or cast doubts on formed opinions and strategies. Combining instinct with research results can prevent an idea or design from falsely being labeled *new* or *wrong* simply because it is *unfamiliar*.

Guts and Glory

When great disparity between research findings and expected findings is encountered, it is wise to pause and retrace the steps that brought the team to the tested solution. It is then time to make a sensible judgment, using *data combined with intuition*, whether the testing truly revealed unforeseen insights or it was somehow misinterpreted or initially misguided. Research showed that Ronald McDonald was going to be a devastating flop as a mascot for Ray Kroc's restaurant chain. Research also showed that no one would watch a feature-length cartoon, nor would they have interest in a theme park, but Walt Disney pressed forward anyway. Gathering insights and validation is tremendously valuable, so get as much as possible. When designers and their clients overlay research data with gut feelings, they have the best odds of coming up with the next big idea or trend.

The smart infusion of packaging science—things like trend analysis, market research and consumer insights—is critical to strategic design. Designers are naturally emotionally involved in the work, but they must also be intellectually immersed in it. The best package design comes from designers who leverage the science of packaging, and marketers who allow freedom of artistic expression in their brands.

We Start at **40,000 FEET** (12,192 M)

[1] What do the consumers **THINK/SEE/FEEL?**
- Do they care? Is the brand/product relevant?
- What do they *say*? (stated feelings/intent)
- What do they *do*? (actual behavior)

[2] Brand/Product **ASSESSMENT** (promise and personality)
- Brand vs. brand
- Brand as expressed across product/line
- Product vs. product

[3] What is their **LIFESTYLE?**
- What's going on in their lives? (active/passive)
- Is the brand/product commensurate?
- Is the positioning a touchpoint?
- Does the visual personality make a connection?

[4] Observations and **CONCLUSIONS**
- What does it all mean?
- Why does it matter?
- Where do we go from here?

Phase 1: The **PACKAGING BRIEF**

Effective packaging briefs not only include several common strategic forms of direction but also exude a pulse or a spirit that transcends mere data and bullet points.

All-too-general packaging briefs are often a challenge. It is common to find briefs that lean toward boilerplate, and they're not helpful.

- Broad age ranges and demographics without an identified "sweet spot," target consumers.
- Clichéd adjectives to describe brand voice; fun, confident, friendly, trustworthy, etc. Some may be correct, but could be true of hundreds of brands. Narrative statements that encapsulate tone and personality are more helpful.
- Generic packaging objectives such as "make it pop," "postured as a leader in category," "clean."

The designer must review the brief from both a strategic and a tactical perspective. Any vagueness, inconsistencies, or direction that doesn't jive with the stated goals should be questioned and discussed during discovery. If necessary, changes should be made to the brief to clarify disparities and finalize the objectives of the packaging project.

ELEMENTS OF A GOOD CREATIVE BRIEF

As a general rule, a solid packaging creative brief should include these elements:

- Product/brand essence and/or voice
- Some measure or scale of desired change from evolutionary to revolutionary
- Package design objectives (sometimes panel-by-panel)
- Target audience identification and demographics
- Top-line consumer attitudes and behaviors
- Gender/age range and sweet spot
- Economic and lifestyle insights
- Communication objectives and hierarchy
- Who am I? What makes me special? Why should you buy me?
- List of current equities (from rigid to flexible)
- Current or desired segmentation breakdown
- Product attributes and distinguishing characteristics
- Competitive overview of rival brands and advantages
- Known or perceived category risks or sensitivities
- Package tech specs
- Current package samples or other supporting visuals
- Timing and milestones

THE BALANCED "YOKE" OF THE CREATIVE BRIEF

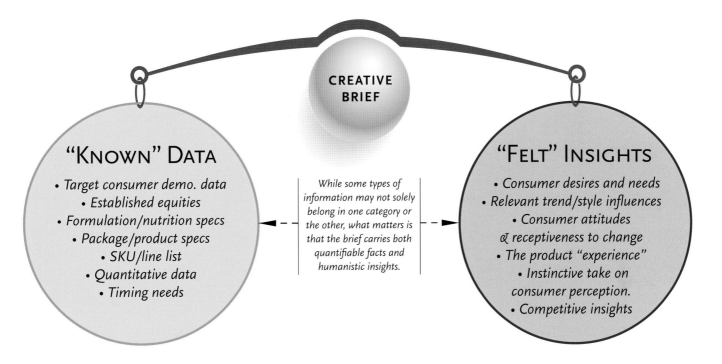

CREATIVE BRIEF

"Known" Data

- Target consumer demo. data
- Established equities
- Formulation/nutrition specs
- Package/product specs
- SKU/line list
- Quantitative data
- Timing needs

While some types of information may not solely belong in one category or the other, what matters is that the brief carries both quantifiable facts and humanistic insights.

"Felt" Insights

- Consumer desires and needs
- Relevant trend/style influences
- Consumer attitudes & receptiveness to change
- The product "experience"
- Instinctive take on consumer perception.
- Competitive insights

Brand Equities

Brand equities are tangible brand attributes that are concretely identifiable and owned to some degree in the product's category. Color, shape, type style, pattern, and texture are common equities that should often be preserved but also possibly played with. Marketers tend to overshelter equities and guard them so closely that they become shackles. Nothing is more boring than a package that never changes with the culture.

Phase 1: Visual **AUDITS**

Visual audits vary widely in scope and intent but have several goals in common.

Step 1

First, effective audits involve surveying multiple environments in which a package is merchandised or promoted. The focus should be on the channels with the greatest exposure to the target consumer, but, when possible, secondary or more obscure locations should be studied as well. Sometimes advantages can be recognized and shares gained in less obvious places. In the primary product arena, objectivity is key when noting strengths and weaknesses. It is also important to observe similar environments in multiple markets. This will help identify common competitive factors and the presence of uncontrollables such as merchandising, lighting, and categorical clutter.

Step 2

Second, an audit should note key environmental factors, ranging from macro to micro, that have impact from the moment a consumer enters a store. Of critical note are the following:

- *Category location within the store.* Hard to find? Impulse? Back of the store?
- *Neighboring product categories.* When observing your product, what's in your periphery? Does it matter?
- *Product slotting within the category.* Central or fringe? Common neighbors? Top shelf or floor level?
- *Scope of direct competition within the category.* Multiple shelves/facings? What do the competitors own (color, messages, package shape, etc)?
- *Multiple SKU/line extensions.* If your product is part of a line, how identifiable are individual SKUs? Do they sufficiently differentiate within your line *and* from the competition?
- *Stopping power.* Does the product stand out or recede? Leader or me-too?
- *Additional marketing factors.* Promotions within the category? Shelf talkers or other merchandising or signage? Noteworthy price disparities with direct competitors?
- *Presence of private label.* Generics, copycats, or premium store brands?

Step 3

Last, reviewing notes and photos immediately after the audit yields optimal depth of perception and helps designers and clients extract the most gut-level responses that can be translated into the most relevant conclusions. The takeaway fades once you leave, so collect your thoughts right away.

Left: Two spreads for the shelf life audit DuPuis conducted for Nestlé Malted Milk include analysis of the old packaging along with a review of in-store shelf positioning.

Top: Style boards assist the client and the creative team in developing a visual language and stylistic approach for the product.

Bottom: The marketing and DuPuis design teams selected these images and words collectively so they could better visualize the Pop-Tart brand persona. That persona was referred to throughout the packaging and branding process.

Phase 2: **MESSAGING** and **COMMUNICATION** Management

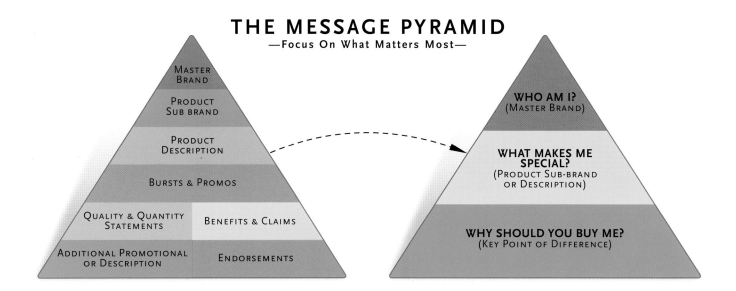

THE MESSAGE PYRAMID
—Focus On What Matters Most—

A well-planned messaging hierarchy involves more than listing features and benefits in order of importance. It must also acknowledge the relationship between various messages. Strictly crafting a package with a message hierarchy represented in order and/or by relative scale will lead to message overload and clutter. When elements are grouped by both sensible copy development and visual compartmentalization, a well-designed package can say all. To help keep messaging effective, each element should speak to the following three agendas:

1. **Vision and purpose:** Who am I?
2. **Conflict and opportunity:** What makes me special?
3. **Reception and acceptance:** Why should you buy me?

Top: The chart (above) shows how too much communication can clutter and distract from the three key messages.

MESSAGING MANAGEMENT

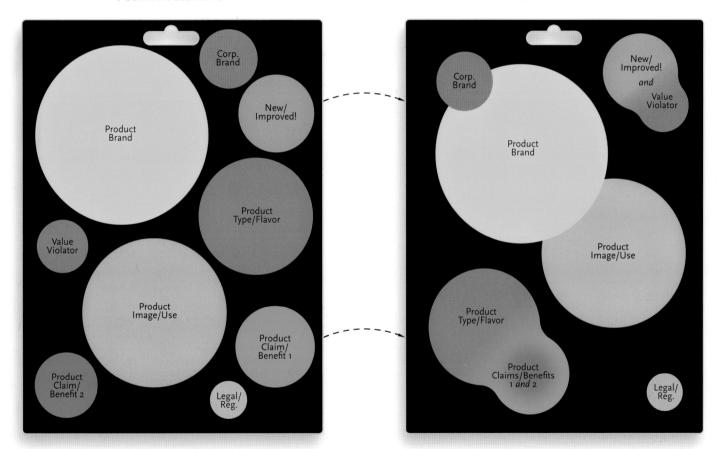

COMMON PDP MESSAGING
9 SEPARATE ELEMENTS

Corp. Brand

New/ Improved!

Product Brand

Value Violator

Product Type/Flavor

Product Image/Use

Product Claim/ Benefit 1

Product Claim/ Benefit 2

Legal/ Reg.

OPTIMIZED MESSAGING
1/3 FEWER PERCEIVED ELEMENTS

New/ Improved! and Value Violator

Corp. Brand

Product Brand

Product Image/Use

Product Type/Flavor

Product Claims/Benefits 1 and 2

Legal/ Reg.

LESS OFTEN MEANS *MORE*, BUT WHEN MORE IS UNAVOIDABLE, CREATE THE ILLUSION OF LESS ON THE PRIMARY DISPLAY PANEL (PDP) OF THE PACKAGE. *First, word-smith message solutions that combine like elements where possible to reduce package clutter. The mind can digest simple compound messages when they have common intent. Remember, what matters most on packaging: "WHO AM I?", "WHAT MAKES ME SPECIAL?", and "WHY SHOULD YOU BUY ME?"*

Phase 2: Visual Interpretation of **THE BRIEF**

Creating package design that achieves the objectives of a brief requires several interpretive disciplines. First the design firm's creative director must be effective at translating the brief into an inspired creative vision for the team. That direction must both harness the creative team's energy toward a targeted solution and allow for the development of an array of packaging solutions that meet and stretch expectations. What is *too far*? The boundary should not lie just at the edge of what's comfortable. Simply hitting the brief with a solution that feels right or looks appropriate often produces more of the same and lacks impact.

Before

Case Study | Skinny Cow

Skinny Cow, a healthful alternative to full-fat ice cream, had a loyal consumer base. To expand its reach and attract new consumers, a redesign was in order along with revitalizing the cow character, but not at the cost of losing its cult following. Above is the package prior to the redesign by DuPuis.

Brainstorming

What do you envision when you close your eyes and imagine a brainstorm? The term implies an indiscriminate variety of thoughts and concepts rapidly swirling around, fueled by the infinite imaginative power of the mind. Starting the storm requires a temporary removal of predetermined barriers and a suspension of conventional thought. In order to come up with new or refreshing ideas, people must set aside common perceptions and expectations. When possible, having designers, creative directors, marketers, and business managers deep dive together at the onset of a new packaging program produces not only a broader array of ideation but also forms a collaborative synergy across multiple disciplines that can fuel positive change (and lower risk aversion) throughout the entire campaign.

After

Concerns to Be Addressed

- **Lack of strategic alignment.** Designers and clients must be clear on the objectives. If any doubts exist, ask, discuss, even challenge, if necessary. Better to probe now than argue later. Also, loose ideations and conceptual approaches can be helpful if offered by the creative team to tactically zero in on the client's goals and expectations.
- **Going too far off-brand** in the name of creativity and violating the brand's DNA.
- **Design iterations rather than multiple designs.** Creatives can be sensitive to visual changes or tweaks and mistake such variances as new design. Be sure to show the agreed number of designs/concepts in the form of truly different designs. Iterations should be strategically justified and not just presentation filler.
- **Too many design options** at this early stage can backfire. An agreed number of designs/comps for first exploration takes into account not only budget considerations but also the client's appetite for creative choices. Presenting dramatically more than the agreed upon number of comps can:

  - Upset the client's confidence that the firm is sure of the goals and objectives
  - Make the firm appear overzealous or not budget conscious
  - Simply take too long to present and be overwhelming to absorb

Left: Initial focus was placed on refining the Skinny Cow brand personality. Who was she to consumers? What potential lay in enhancing her role on the package? The design exploration included Skinny the Cow in a variety of expressive roles integrated within the logotype.

Over the following pages, see DuPuis' step-by-step redesign process for Skinny Cow.

Phase 2: Conceptual **IDEATIONS**

Early concept development and ideation is best shown in black-and-white sketch form. Sketches provide just enough visual information to communicate an idea, graphic architecture, and space planning. Such roughs force people to look beyond specifics. Keeping an early focus on the root idea allows the conceptual cement to dry as a solid foundation for the steps ahead. Jumping to tight color concepts right out of the gate does the package and brand a disservice by changing this vitally strategic stage into a beauty contest. It is all too common to find a potentially great concept rejected because of subjectively incorrect execution, while a weaker concept may be selected because it has a more appealing graphic treatment. Dealing with client-side packaging teams that have little background in graphic development/management or sufficient exposure to visual arts can be challenging. Their lack of experience means they may want tighter comps immediately. The potentially harmful outcome is a design system that lacks depth, meaning, and, ultimately, effectiveness. Key tools in the designer's toolbox that are shown to support sketches:

- **Color.** Suitable or established palettes that aid in shopability and ownership.
- **Linking elements.** Visual elements that either literally or conceptually tie multiple products into a family.
- **Graphic architecture.** The collective balance and composition of visual elements and messaging.
- **Photography.** Powerful descriptive and emotive potential that can be either in the background or the foreground.
- **Typography.** Style and character via letter forms has an impact far deeper than the literal meaning of the words they form.
- **Brand hierarchy.** Strategic relationship between brand, sub-brand, and segment name through flavor or product description.

Selected brand mark sketches were taken to color to further identify and confirm directional approaches.

Rough conceptual approaches allow ideas to freely be explored without the commitment of hours in implementing a full-color concept. The client and the design team thus have time to focus on the objectives more clearly before being involved in color and graphic treatments.

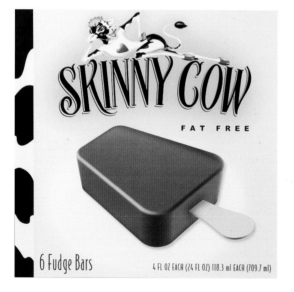

Upon client review of the packaging sketches, DuPuis then proceeded to develop these full color comps.

A Word About Typography

One huge distinction that sets a strategic design firm apart from other creative shops is its perspective on typography. Especially as it pertains to branding and core messaging, typography is not simply the process of choosing a font. It is the craft of communicating emotion, attitude, and various forms of value declaration via letterforms and words. A design firm's typographical prowess is not proportionate to the size of the font library it owns, but rather its understanding of type as a life-form whose infinite strains are in constant evolution. If not completely crafted from scratch, designers' font choices when developing a brand are more like hand picking fabrics for a suit; they are chosen for their tactile feel and strength, but it still takes a gifted tailor to shape the fabric and transform it into the ultimate fit.

A variety of typographic sensibilities expressed here includes DuPuis' Above & Beyond cream cheese (top), Partner Design's bakery products (bottom, left), IMA Design's men's grooming aids (bottom, middle), and Iaga's packaging for jellies and jams (bottom, right).

Phase 3: **REFINEMENT**

R efinement is the combined process of maximizing the effectiveness of a design direction and validating the direction itself. Strategies take tactical form, and ideas become executions. Most of the time, refinement involves taking preliminary sketches to a more tangible form. Solid concepts are often difficult for clients to choose among until they have been executed to a visual state that is closer to what the consumer will see. When time and budget allow, research can be used to validate choices.

On Strategy

It is vital to keep the brief front and center when reviewing design, because it is easy to forget *why* and become entranced by *how*. Sometimes refinement can become more about beautification than a proper translation of strategy into visual language.

Preproduction

As a best practice, it is vital to engage the production partners—that is, separators, printers, and fabricators—as early in the design process as possible. The designers should know the printing process and/or production limitations involved in the project. Often near the end of the refinement stage,

a preproduction (pre-pro) meeting is held to reveal the design to those who will be charged with reproducing it.

In this meeting, all parties should have digital or hard copies of the design to review and discuss. It is important to inform all back-end process partners of the program's strategic goals so they can make technical recommendations and edits. There are often many ways to solve reproduction concerns; likewise, there is often a best approach that optimizes current systems to achieve best results. It is the responsibility of both designer and client to keep strategy at the forefront.

Three directions were selected for further refinement. At this stage, the focus was on optimizing communication elements and defining the visual architecture.

Planogram Views

How will the consumer see the new package? One thing is for sure: It won't be beautifully output on high-end photo paper, mounted on a black matte board, and displayed under presentation lighting in a conference room. It will be on-shelf and subjected to environmental factors such as slotting position, low or bad lighting, the competition, and merchandising attention. It is also exposed to itself (depending on how many facings or SKUs are involved).

It is vital to look at a package design in planogram form to simulate the manner in which it will be encountered by the consumer. Cumulative effects and billboarding dynamics occur when products are arranged according to their ultimate planogram; these must be previewed.

Dominant color equities express ownership or leadership in a category and how well a design communicates Who am I?, What am I?, and Why should you buy me? are valuable perspectives gained when viewing planogram simulations. We recommend doing planograms (or shelf-sets) as early in the package development process as is reasonable.

Phase 4: Final **REFINEMENTS** and **LINE EXTENSION**

The goal of the refinement phase is ideally to select a singular design direction that has gained approval by the client for both content and visual execution.

Application Rollout

While legal standards and regulatory mandates may require adjustments, it is in the implementation stage that a design is applied to an entire line or product segment. This process may involve rolling out the smallest of iterations in the form of size and quantity changes, or it may include the develop ment of several layers of line extensions. The scope of implementation may embrace major color variations, sub-brand treatments, and adjustments to the established master architecture to aid in segmentation—even a variety of structures and forms. In these larger-scale situations, the approach to these variants is addressed in the previous refinement stage by developing representative product samples from throughout the line to test the scalability of the design system. The time to realize a package design cannot support the range of products involved is *not* in implementation.

Common Pitfall

One pitfall commonly observed is too casual or formulaic an approach to implementation. There is an erroneous perspective that once the master design system is approved, the rest is just plug and play. What we have found, though, is that any remaining product or SKU to be deployed may have a life and sometimes a consumer of its own. If the manner in which it is executed pays any less attention to detail or if the customization needed to optimize the design for that SKU is overlooked, the result could be failure rather than success.

Before

After

Case Study

The before and after show clearly how photography can play an important role in establishing product quality and brand positioning. The redesign by DuPuis enhanced the product's home-cooked appearance, resulting in an over 20 percent rise in sales.

Back panels serve as a place for consumers to further involve themselves with the brand, before and after purchase. These panels are also the location for information on the product's ingredients and nutritional information. Careful consideration must be given to the balance of product information and brand story.

Phase 5: File **PRODUCTION**

Don't fumble on the 1-yard line. Think through production. Unfortunately, prepress and printing are sometimes left to be managed by someone other than the designer. However, it is best if the designer stays involved in the supervising the process.

File Preparation

It is nearly impossible to put into words how files should be prepared for final output because best practices vary wildly depending on client-vendor dynamics. Terms such as *production* and *mechanical* have been pivotal in the graphic design lexicon for many decades, but their meanings have been so diluted and stretched that they are no longer clearly defined. Digital technologies have blurred, if not erased, the delineation of roles between designer and printer. When clients request 'mechanicals,' they may mean completely finalized art that needs no further modification and can be ripped directly to plates for printing, or they may want working design files that have FPO elements, preliminary color assignments, and temporary dielines, but lack the fine tuning needed to yield viable output for printing purposes.

Smart designers are becoming more and more knowledgeable about production, and printers are becoming better designers.

For the sake of this book, *file preparation* refers to the agreed condition of art as it passes hands from the design firm to the separator. This agreement is established in the preproduction meeting in which the roles and responsibilities of the design firm and the printer/separator are clearly defined.

Who will:

- Ensure brand standard compliance?
- Drop in final legal and regulatory data?
- Digitally separate the art according to the color/ink specs?
- Adjust color densities appropriate to the specific process/press?
- Run color proofs and provide required color targets?
- Execute other pre-press measures such as trapping and imposition?

You are only as good as your last mistake, so if a designer allows a client to experience headaches and tumult at the end of a job, even if it's not "your job," you have let the client down. Plan, communicate, and be the conduit of proactive discussions that review the prospective design and all the what-ifs.

Color Correction

With all the advancements caused by the digital revolution, one party to the production process is still the stopgap for correct color. Assuming that printers operate within an acceptable margin of color assurance and accuracy, whoever handles the digital art last before plate-making is responsible. It is incumbent on the separator to understand through preliminary color proofs what the design firm and marketing team expect the outcome to be. The separator also must interface with the printer to interpret and appropriately modify the provided art to fit the press tolerances, media limitations, and process specs (e.g., dot gain, registration, analog ratings, ink behaviors) so the art ultimately reproduces accurately. It is common for printers to do their own separation work for these reasons because no one knows their presses like they do.

The design firm is responsible for getting the color close enough to eliminate improvisation and interpretation. The better a design firm understands prepress and printing, the smoother the final art handoff will be.

Pre-Pro Checklist

Client: _____ **Job #:** _____

Description: _____

1. DESIGN APPROVAL

Date of Design Approval:_____
Approved orm: ❑ PDF ❑ Hard Copy ❑ Mock-up
Design/Comp version:_____
_____

2. TIMELINE

1st mech date to client:_____
Special routing needs?_____
  (eg. legal review, license partners, director go-ahead, etc)
Deadline to separator:_____
Approx. press date:_____
DuPuis to attend? ❑ Yes ❑ No

3. PRE-PRESS SPECS

Separator name & contact:_____
_____
Printer name & contact:_____
_____
Print process: ❑ Offset ❑ Roto ❑ Flexo ❑ Digital ❑ Screen
Dieline provided/confirmed:_____
Color space: ❑ CMYK ❑ RGB ❑ GS ❑ Other_____
Spot color channels needed in PS?: ❑ Yes ❑ No
Imposition or step/repeats?:_____
Default resolution: _____
Min type/KO reqs:_____
Ink lineup:_____
_____
Special inks or effects?:_____
Min dot & max desnsity reqs:_____
Digital seps by whom?:_____
Color Targets to be provided by DuPuis? ❑ Yes ❑ No
  If yes, type and source:_____
Agreed software/version:_____

4. IMAGE/LAYOUT REQUIREMENTS

Photography/Illustrations: ❑ Done ❑ Needed
  If needed, from whom?_____
Final hires composed by:_____
Final color edits by:_____
Any FPO elements?:_____
Legal requirements:_____
  (eg. ®'s, TM's, Kosher symbols, etc)
Product codes/UPC numbers:_____
Other Corporate mandatories?_____
_____

5. ART RELEASE & DELIVERY

❑ FTP ❑ CD/DVD ❑ Online ❑ Other
To whom?:_____

6. Notes

_____
_____
_____
_____

BE BOLD

BE CREATIVE

BE A LEADER

This mechanical for the Skinny Cow Skinny Carb Ice Cream Bars shows the complexity of the package's printing specifications. DuPuis had numerous preproduction meetings with their client, the separator, and the printer in order to troubleshoot the potential separation and reproduction issues.

The Purpose of Pre-Pro

1. Identify the overall reproductive feasibility of the design before it is finalized. Incorporate agreed upon accommodations that best utilize available systems.

2. Establish clear lines of production and prepress responsibilities among the various parties. Who will compose final imagery? Who will strip the digital color separations? How will color targets be provided, and by whom? In what condition should the files be handed over from the design firm? How should the art release be handled?

3. Identify technical details. What are the established specifications for the structural and/or printed materials involved? Consider substrate pros and cons, number of available inks, dielines, press tolerances, and so on.

4. Confirm timing and delivery expectations.

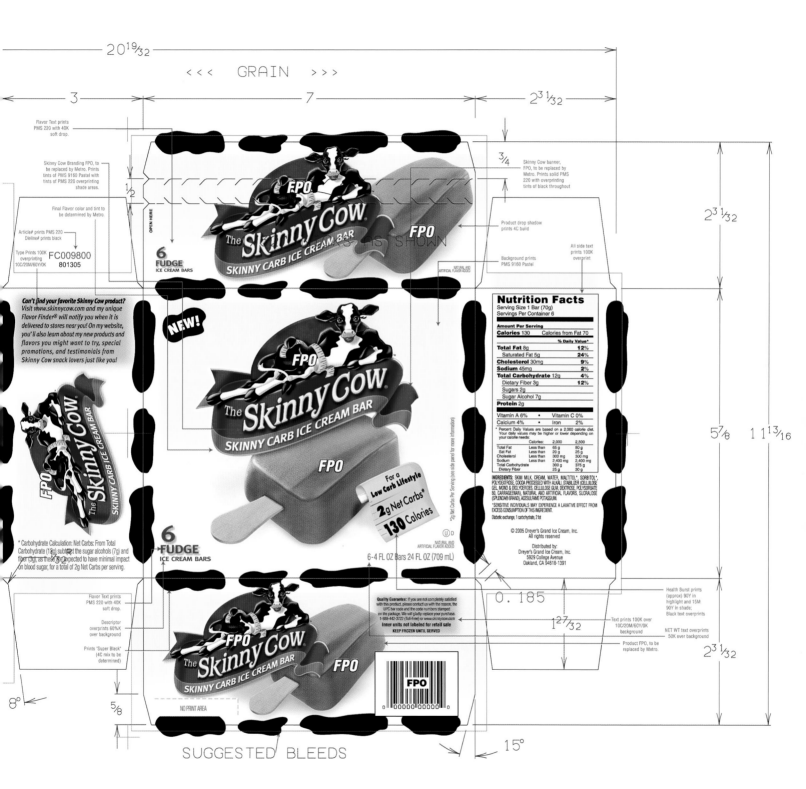

Phase 5: Standards and **STYLE GUIDES**

To leverage the investment made in developing effective packaging for a product line, a plan is needed for near future line extensions or new innovations. That plan is set forth in a packaging standards or style guide. In short, standards guides identify rigid guidelines regarding the scale and position of branding and other visual elements, font usage, color palettes, application of trade dress, and empirical do's and don'ts that prevent grotesque errors in future adaptations.

A standards guide is instrumental in providing brand equity controls over package design implementation and adaptations. Style guides, on the other hand, are farther-reaching in creative scope because they provide more background to a packaging system's style and aesthetic intent. Style guides ensure the spirit of a package design is considered, applied, and evolved correctly when developing new product segments so a common vision is applied throughout design and execution.

Care and Maintenance: Asset Management

Integral to the future application and leveraging of current packaging standards is the role of sophisticated asset management. Without a substantial asset management system, packaging managers are relegated to storing, locating, and copying CD-ROMs or paying fees to their vendor partners to pull previous designs and standard elements for new initiatives.

An online asset management tool or intuitive digital repository helps ensure that standard assets are available for repurposing. These systems require the ongoing attention of a "cybrarian" or system manager, and usually require a significant capital investment in either an outside service or hardware and software, their benefits dramatically offset the costs. Such systems also grow exponentially more powerful and valuable in the packaging process as time goes on and more assets are contributed.

However, of greatest import to an asset management system's success is that it is deployed correctly and maintained with great diligence as it grows.

A style guide, as seen to the left, is an effective way to assure that branding and packaging will maintain their integrity. The document should give examples of line extensions and areas for promotional violators along with brand placement.

Right: The finished package design for Skinny Cow

MASTERING THE ART OF
PACKAGE DESIGN

*Translating goals and vision into
form, function, and style*

Six **PURPOSES** of Packaging

This book discusses many of packaging's reasons for being and how packaging has evolved into a strategic touchpoint with consumers. This vital work and background becomes a vision that ultimately translates into a package on a shelf. To get there, seemingly countless decisions about packaging form and function must be made that factor in product demands, shape, material, marketing communication, and final execution. Every step of the process must be taken with the original objectives in mind. Each package must be executed consistent with brand positioning and must go beyond consumer expectations to delight them.

1. **Containment.** How will the package hold the product? Liquids, chemicals, dense solids, perishable foods and pharmaceuticals, exceedingly small or oversized items, and high-tech and high-cost goods all have unique needs and varying demands on the containers that secure them.

2. **Security.** Does the product require special tamper evidence or sanitary and freshness measures? From oxygen barriers to holographic security seals, many packages must afford special assurances to both manufacturer and consumer.

3. **Protection.** How easily can the product be damaged in transit or handling? How well can it withstand environmental factors? Damaged or spoiled product is pure material and economic waste. Packages must address strength and protection needs in a product-by-product manner.

4. **Convenience.** Can the package make the product easier to transport, display, open, close, use, or reuse? In many categories that are or approach being commodities, the issue of consumer convenience is paramount. A smart package takes end-user needs into account and provides often unexpected solutions, thus giving the product an edge to the marketplace.

5. **Information.** How do you provide the consumer with the knowledge to understand and use a product? Packaging bears the huge responsibility of informing the consumer of what a product is for, how to use it and when, how *not* to use it, and why not.

6. **Marketing.** What means should you employ to elevate the consumer's purchase intent? Speaking the right visual language on-pack that connects intellectually and emotionally with the consumer is vital to getting a product noticed, desired, purchased, and remembered.

Right: Some standard containers illustrate the wide variety of packaging choices available.

Structural Design: **PAPER** or **PLASTIC**?

The choice of material for any given package was once driven almost exclusively by *needs*—for appropriate containment, environmental durability, freshness, stability—and by available resources. Today addressing those needs is intensely scientific and has become a massive industry in itself. Compounding the choices now are *wants*. The consumer wants convenient features, improved portability, ease of use, improved value, and even style and entertainment qualities.

Needs and Wants

Functional structure designs that satisfy the most demanding needs yet appeal to the consumer's ever-evolving list of wants now seem to be the cost of entry into most markets. Ironically we are now seeing structural trends that bring us back to need. However, the new need comes not from the product but from the earth—a desire for sustainability. Public consciousness of resource depletion, waste, and social responsibility is gaining momentum. In other words,

the purpose of structural package design has slowly expanded from simple function to include desire and now aspects of survival as well.

Trend and Innovation

There is a reason why many categories of consumer products are dominated by one particular structural trend over another. Trends are usually dictated by function but driven by competition and price sensitivity. In other words, while you can't package milk with a hangtag,

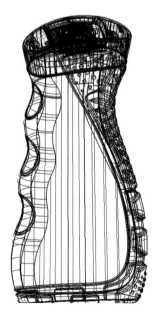

CAD drawings of Axe shower gel by Just Blue Design show the complexity of structural design and engineering.

you can't afford to sell it in a crystal carafe, either. However, within the milk market, you will find HDPE plastic jugs, coated paper gable-top cartons, Tetra boxes, and, yes, even glass. Technological innovation drives the quest for new and more effective or efficient materials. Product innovation drives the need for new technologies. In some cases, the package is so innovative and consumer-minded that it becomes the product rather than simply its container.

The more of a commodity your product is, the more packaging can play a role in significant differentiation. Of course, price sensitivity is relevant as well, but the right design can engage consumers afresh and spark increased interest as a product becomes more integral to lifestyle and true benefits.

Materials Criteria

Manufacturers go through their own processes to decide how to select a material, but here are the major considerations:

- What's best for my consumer?
- What's best for my product?
- What's best for my margins?
- Do I/can I own a shape or delivery mechanism? Can I find a better way to do it?
- Should I differentiate through structural innovation?

Structuring Desire

Innovative packaging design can poke at and amplify consumer needs and wants; fun (Squid Soap by Pentagram), desire (Microsoft Vista by Smart Design), trust (GR Motor Oil by Studio One Eleven) can all be achieved through structural cues that don't necessarily require innovative materials. The integration of structural choices and graphic design elements is at the core of all great examples. These points of difference sometimes have little to do with true product advantages yet they make the product stand out, create desire, and say "buy me".

SUSTAINABILITY: Can I Be Green? How Do I Do It?

Authenticity is the key. Nothing can destroy a brand faster than distrust. Consumers are getting more and more savvy about ecological issues, organic production, and the meaning of related certifications. The definition of *sustainability* is a moving target and changes dramatically depending on whether you're listening to a concerned consumer or Wal-Mart. The Sustainable Packaging Coalition defines it as "cradle-to-cradle principles dedicated to transforming packaging into a system that encourages economic prosperity and a sustainable flow of materials utilizing renewable resources within a program that sees to it, benefiting the people/region from where the resources/manufacturing come, and a responsible approach to waste both in volume and nature."

Is Sustainable Attainable?

If the Earth calling out for change isn't enough, designers can be sure that as the consumer continues to demand it, marketers will listen. However, there is, naturally, a time lapse between the birth of green and its widespread adoption. Once the idea of being green transfers from the head, where it is a good idea, to the heart, where it becomes a value, the consumer's dollar will dictate supply options through real demand.

Concern and eco-awareness are growing, and the packaging industry is responding by examining what's being done now and exploring new opportunities to improve current tandards. Some manufacturers are taking the lead toward both optimizing the packaging life cycle and exercising greater social responsibility.

Environmentally sensitive packaging for Cargo cosmetics: The Cargo products' materials are embedded with plant seed so that, when discarded, the package sprouts plants—a beautiful way to recycle.

1.

2.

3.

4.

5.

6.

7.

1. **Tiger Friendly**
   Animal Preservation, Economic Development
2. **USDA—Organic**
   U.S. Department of Agriculture Certified
   Organic
3. **Salmon Safe**
   Sustainable Agriculture
4. **Food Alliance (FA)**
   Pest Management, Social
   Responsibility, Sustainable Agriculture
5. **Fair Trade Certified**
   Pest Management, Social
   Responsibility, Sustainable Agriculture
6. **Rainforest Alliance Certified**
   Pest Management, Social
   Responsibility, Sustainable Agriculture
7. **Certified Vegan**
   Animal Welfare, Sustainable Agriculture

The Definition of Sustainable Packaging

The Sustainable Packaging Coalition notes the following—that sustainable packaging:

- Is beneficial, safe, and healthy—for individuals and communities throughout its life cycle
- Meets market criteria for performance and cost
- Is sourced, manufactured, transported, and recycled using renewable energy.
- Maximizes the use of renewable or recycled source materials
- Is manufactured using clean production technologies and best practices.
- Is made from materials healthy in all probable end-of-life scenarios
- Is physically designed to optimize materials and energy
- Is effectively recovered and utilized in biological and/or industrial cradle-to-cradle cycles

Eco-Icons and Certifications

More ways are being sought to assure consumers of product safety and sustainable manufacturing. Icons, stamps of approval, and certifications of authenticity are popping up and shouting "Trust me!" Truth and substantiation are the costs of entry, so organizations are taking steps to elevate awareness of their causes.

PACKAGE TYPE	TECHNICAL/PRODUCTION NOTES
Bottle/Container (plastic) Small containers used most often to store liquids. Usually made by a blow-molding process.	**Materials:** **PET** (polyethylene terphthalate) Strong, transparent, inexpensive, lightweight, shatter resistance, and recyclable. Less reactive to permeable gas, so liquids retain carbonation **PE** (polyethylene) Comes in high (HDPE), medium (MDPE), and low (LDPE) density. The higher the density, the more rigid the container. **HDPE** (high density polyethylene) Most widely used plastic. Economical, impact resistant, and good moisture barrier. Compatible with a range of acids and caustics, but not with solvents. **PVC** (polyvinyl chloride) Naturally clear, extremely resistant to oils, resists most gasses, good drop impact **P/P** (polypropylene) Similar to HDPE, except that it is more transparent (but not as clear as PET or PVC). **Printing:** Silkscreening, various label technologies
Bottle/Jar (glass) Small containers used most often to store liquids. A small container that often has a neck narrower than the body. The top or mouth of a bottle is closed by a bottle cap or stopper.	**Materials:** **Type I Glass** is made from borosilicate, that are highly resistant and release little alkali. Commonly used for pharmaceutical or fine chemical products that are sensitive to PH changes **Type II Glass** is made from commercial soda lime glass that is dealkalized to improve chemical resistance. This treatment etches the surface, causing a frosted appearance. **Type III Glass** is made of untreated commercial soda-lime glass which has somewhat above-average chemical resistance. The most commonly used type, it is compatible with most items it is filled with. **Type NP Glass** is untreated and made of ordinary soda-lime glass that is unsuitable for holding most products.

USAGE	EXAMPLE

Typical uses: Water, soft drinks, oil (cooking and fuel), shampoo, cleaning products, personal care products

Benefits of plastic include versatility, extreme durability, flexibility in tailoring to specific technical needs, lightweight relative to many competing materials (requires less fuel to transport), resistance to chemicals, water, and impact. Good safety and hygiene properties for food packaging. Relatively inexpensive to produce

A popular variation: A specialty spray bottle with a dispensing system to create an aerosol mist of a liquid

Typical uses: Wine, soft drinks, oil, beer, soup, vegetables, liquid medicine, pharmaceuticals, perfume, ink, personal care products

Glass maintains a product's freshness for long periods, lengthening shelf life. When colored, especially amber or green, it can protect light-sensitive items. Glass is hygienic, providing a high degree of sterilization. It is impermeable so leakage is impossible, unless inadequately sealed, and it contains strong odors. It is compatible with a variety of labeling technologies and is highly recyclable.

PACKAGE TYPE	TECHNICAL/PRODUCTION NOTES
Can (tin) An air-tight container made of thin metal that requires cutting or tearing to open. Called a can, tin can, or tin, these containers hold a variety of products, with the overwhelming majority being food preserved by canning.	**Materials:** No longer made of tin, cans are fabricated with aluminum or steel. Typically cans have a printed paper or plastic label glued to the outside cylinder body. Less common is printing directly on the metal. Most cans are fabricated in three pieces—flat top, bottom, and cylindrical body. Usually have a rim at top and bottom that is a slightly larger diameter than the can body. Milk products are canned with a nearly rimless construction.
Beverage Can Most often an aluminum can that holds a single serving of a beverage. Typically has a pull-tab opening in the top, which is actually a stay-tab because it is not pulled off, to dispense the liquid. Sometimes retailed separately, but often sold as six packs or boxed in twelve or twenty-four pack cases.	**Materials:** **Aluminum:** In most parts of the world, beverage cans may be returned for a deposit and be recycled. Aluminum recycling is cost effective and readily available. Some consumers find that the beverage cans cause a change in taste and also believe that aluminum leaching into the beverage can be dangerous to their health. Aluminum's relation to Alzheimer's Disease is being studied and debated.
Carton (specialty) Boxes can be created in a variety of specific shapes and usages. Various geometric shapes including rectangles, squares, ovals, and rounds can be designed specifically to hold a particular product.	**Materials:** **Aluminum and steel:** Not so eco-friendly, aerosols have health concerns because of deliberate inhaling of the contents to provide a high propellant, as well as the fact that other dangerous chemicals and particles can piggyback into the human respiratory system.

USAGE	EXAMPLE
Typical uses: Vegetables, fruits, milk, nuts, soup, fish, engine oil, pet food Come in assorted sizes. Steel cans are very recyclable. Self-heating cans are multichambered, the inner one holds the product, and the outer ones holds chemicals that react when combined. By pulling a ring on the can, the barrier separating the chemicals in the outer chamber breaks, and the can heats to warm the food.	
Typical uses: Soda, beer. Holds carbonated liquids under pressure very well. **Standard sizes:** North America is 12 fluid ounces (355 ml), India and Europe 330 ml, Australia 375 ml, South Africa 340 ml. An internal coating protects the container from its contents. Aluminum is strong, durable, and very light. It provides excellent barrier protection against air, light, and micro organisms all of which preserves contents. Aluminum packages are secure, tamper proof, hygienic, and easy to open.	
Typical uses: Cooking spray, deodorants, insecticides, and paints. **How it works:** With the contents under pressure, when this container's valve is opened by pressing down the spray button, the liquid product is forced out of a small hole in a fine mist.	

PACKAGE TYPE	TECHNICAL/PRODUCTION NOTES
Bleached paperboard (SBS) Used widely in the food and consumer goods industries. Extremely flexible, great for printing, and environmentally advantageous.	**Materials:** Premium paperboard grade that is produced in a furnace containing at least 80 percent virgin-bleached wood pulp. Most SBS is clay-coated to improve its printing surface and may also be polyethylene-coated for wet strength food packaging. **Printing:** Typically offset lithography
Corrugated box (folding carton) Highly variable corrugated containers, typically rectangular or square. Top is opened by raising the lid, which may or may not be hinged and have a tab closure for resealing.	**Materials:** Typically made of paperboard, usually known as cardboard. May be recycled. Can be waxed or coated with polyethene to seal against moisture. **Colors:** Kraft or white **Printing:** Usually flexography and varous labeling technologies
Carton (specialty) Boxes can be created in a variety of specific shapes and usages. Various geometric shapes including rectangles, squares, ovals, and rounds can be designed specifically to hold a particular product.	**Materials:** Typically made of paperboard, sometimes recycled, which is usually known as cardboard. Specialty cartons can also be made of various plastics including styrofoam and most recently, PET. PS (polystyrene) is often used for egg cartons, fast-food trays, cups, compact disc jackets, and for dry products like vitamins, petroleum jellies, and spices. PS offers excellent clarity and stiffness at an economical cost. It does not provide good barrier properties and has poor impact resistance.

USAGE	EXAMPLE
Typical uses: Bleached paperboard is primarily used for folding cartons, milk cartons, and other packaging products that require superior folding, scoring, and printing characteristics. SBS is also used for disposable cups and plates, food containers, and preprint linerboard for high-graphic corrugated boxes and displays. Some mills that produce SBS packaging board also manufacture lightweight bleached bristols, used by commercial printers for paperback book covers, telephone directory covers, greeting cards, postcards, baseball cards, and merchant displays.	
Typical uses: Innumerable—from fresh produce shipped in bulk to furniture and computer hardware. The Paperboard Packaging Council (PPC) *Ideas and Innovation Handbook* offers over 160 pages with about 250 basic folding carton designs and variations. Die-cut folded box styles include tuck-top mailer, tuck-top mailer with flaps, straight tuck, reverse tuck, tuck top with snap bottom, gable top, self-locking tray.	
Typical uses: Specialty cartons include those for eggs, milk (with or without plastic pouring spout), juice. Tube and tray-style cartons are created for myriad items. Telescoping cartons, where the box is opened by sliding the lid upwards, are often used for cosmetics.	

PACKAGE TYPE	TECHNICAL/PRODUCTION NOTES
Bag Pouches that hold products. Design features include gussets for high volume content, handles, stand-ups, hanging holes for display, and resealable openings with zip-locks.	**Materials:** Can be made of a variety of papers and plastics, both heavy duty for sustained usage/storage, or thin for quick usage and easy recycling. Plastic bags typically use fewer materials than boxes, cans, or jars. Woven polypropylene bags have better burst strength than regular plastic bags and don't degrade when wet. Cellulose is also available. **Printing:** Flexography or rotogravure
Blister pack Blister packs or blisters are preformed clear plastic packages that have a plastic blister top and a printed paperboard or foil backing that are heat sealed together.	**Materials:** PVC, PET, PRET, styrene, HDPE Pharmaceutical blister packs are created by a form-fill-seal process. Rolls of flat film are formed with cavities to fit the product. The cavities are filled, topped with a card or foil, and then sealed—all on the same equipment, called a blisterline. **Printing:** Flexography or silkscreen
Clamshell A more secure type of blister pack. Consists of a paperboard, with the product on it, sandwiched by a clear plastic top and bottom that is heat-sealed together on the edges.	**Materials:** Antistatic, static dissipative, static shielding, and conductive Clamshells can be made in a range of plastics, and are offered in stock as well as custom configurations.
Wrappers Generally refers to a flat sheet made out of paper, cellophane, or plastic that encloses various kinds of packages	**Materials:** **Polyethylene:** Can be embossed **PVC:** Food wrap **LDPE:** Shrink-wrap **Paper:** Various labels

USAGE	EXAMPLE
Typical uses: Frozen food, fresh produce, snack food, candy, cheese, cold meats, gardening products **Bags in Boxes:** Bags made of aluminum PET film or other plastics hold liquids that are packaged within a corrugated cardboard box. This packaging allows for convenience, easy storage, and protects the contents from the elements, such as oxidation of wine.	
Typical uses: Small consumer goods and pharmaceuticals, especially over-the-counter (OTC) products such as tablets, capsules, or lozenges. The main use is packaging individual doses. Blister packs can resist tampering and dispense the product by pushing it through the backing.	
Typical uses: Small theft-prone items, especially toys, hardware, and small electronics. The product can be seen clearly and is held snugly in place. Clamshells are designed to be difficult to open.	
Typical uses: Candy, clothing, cigars, books, food, small items **Shrinkwrap:** A polymer film that shrinks tightly over a product when heated. **Skin Packs:** A product is placed on a paperboard, then a thin sheet of plastic is placed over and heat sealed. **Bellybands:** Used to hold loose things together or partially wrap a box	

GRAPHIC DESIGN:
"Oh, What to Wear?"

Packaging and brand design experts need to understand target consumers inside and out. They need to be on the lookout for new trends that might affect the brands—not only in the design community, but on a global and socio-cultural scale as well. Of course, they must fully understand the business objectives for the brand.

Typographical Mastery

More than simply applying fonts or typefaces, typography is the craft of selecting, customizing, creating, and integrating type solutions. A great deal of personality and emotion can be communicated through typography. Beyond the words and sentences the letters form, type can express elegance or distaste, strength or frailty, rage or tranquility, indulgence or caution, and anything in between. Mediocre typography can deflate even the best package design. Similarly, brilliant typography can produce successful results when almost everything else is lacking.

Brand Ownership

Brand and product recognition are multisensory phenomena. They are usually triggered by visual stimulation but can certainly involve the other senses. Most often in packaging, what you own in a given category is connected to shape, color, a number, and/or a written word. There is also a growing push through packaging innovation to own other qualities such as texture, shine, and even scent.

All these basic elements can be linked either overtly or subconsciously to emotions and implied meanings. If a designer can help form an emotional bond with consumers through a combination of these ownable attributes and the larger brand experience, the result is a connection that can stand up to outside influences such as competitive innovations and price fluctuations.

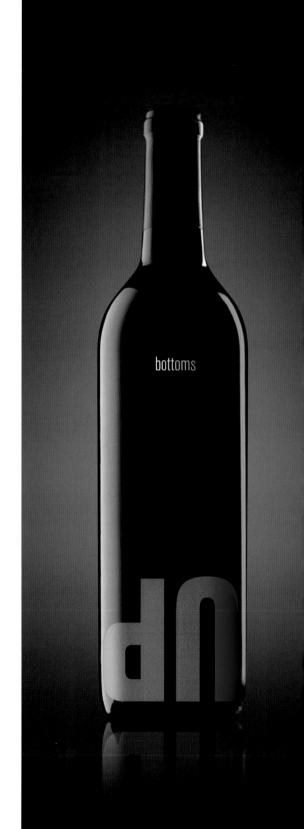

Bottoms UP wine by Wallace Church shows a bold typographic use; Bitter Truth Vodka by Real Pro wraps the product in a newspaper, giving it a handmade feel; and Root: 1 by Turner Duckworth presents typography as a graphic element, along with telling a story.

Visual **LANGUAGES** Morph over Time

Market research on long-life power brands can often bring back consumer impressions that lean toward "stale," "outdated," "flat," or "boring." This trap is often set by marketers themselves as a result of overcommitting to every equity and graphic element as if they are timeless. It's true that some things should remain the same for permanence and staying power, but the ongoing approach to visual languages—the summation of all aspects of the design—must evolve. If it does not, cultural irrelevance and obsolescence are inevitable. Change itself is, therefore, not proportionate to risk. However, an unwillingness to change and evolve a design is far more likely to lead to lack of consumer interest.

Photography or Illustration?

The use of imagery on packaging can be as vital as the branding or messaging. Imagery can be used (among other things) to:

- Demonstrate use
- Express unique innovation
- Create appetite appeal
- Align a product with style/cultural trends
- Invoke desired emotions
- Dispel market paradigms
- Directly relate to a specific demographic

Image type and execution choice vary as much as the purpose. Examples are largely broken into two categories: photography and illustration. Choosing the correct visual approach is driven by several key factors:

- Nature of product category (e.g., electronics, food and beverage, pharmacy)
- Brand essence and personality (e.g., honest/scientific versus trendy/fun)
- Competitive trends (What are the other guys doing? Should we comply or contrast?)
- Value perception (What treatment elevates purchase intent best?)

Before

After

Photography and Appetite Appeal

Appetite appeal sounds specific to food packaging, but the term is more broadly applied. It is tied to food because we associate the word *appetite* with hunger for sustenance. In truth, appetite appeal is the attractive quality of an image that appeals to our hunger for *anything*. When imagery makes us drool over the idea of a product or the experience it provides, the only thing that separates us from satisfying that appetite is the purchase of the product.

Trends in most product categories indicate an evolving taste driven by cultural influences. What looked appetizing ten years ago may not work well on the shelf today because styles change. What was tasty then is often flat or dated now. Currently a bright, more organic style is the rage—but this too is sure to evolve into the next trend.

Left and opposite: As the health and wellness movement grew, so did the look of the bakery category. These examples, designed by DuPuis, demonstrates the changing positioning of consumer desire. Product presentation and typographic elements changed to express a more home-baked feel.

The **BRAND CASCADE**: Credibility or Confusion?

When we use the term *extension*, we assume it refers to a lateral or downward progression of a brand into sub-brands or additional line scale. In reality, branded product lines often extend upward (super- versus sub-branding), typically as a result of acquisition by a new parent company that wants to put its identity on the package as well. This can present a challenge. Consumers may be confused or alienated by this additional branding.

When to Superbrand

When should you superbrand? Many factors enter into this decision, but the choice is typically advantageous when:

- Connection to a previous parent brand must be dissolved due to less-than-positive public perception or a failing brand impression.
- A brand must be reinvigorated, and a parent brand change lends credibility and a fresh start.
- Planned innovations within the brand cannot be adequately supported by the current brand alone.
- Legal ownership requires it. This should be done in a minimalist fashion to satisfy the attorneys without perplexing the consumer.

When to Sub-Brand

- When a true point of difference is being deployed within a brand family that is either broad in scope (SKU count), or so significantly innovative the sub-brand virtually becomes a new product or subset of the parent product brand.

- When a line is getting too wide in scale and sensible segmentation can be achieved through the sub-branding of uniquely grouped offerings. These groupings should only be made if they directly benefit the consumer, increase shopability, or clearly indicate a noteworthy difference in offerings.

No one wants to see a family tree on a package. Corporate brand leaders should be careful not to overestimate the value of their presence on the face of their individual brands, especially if it has done great until now without it.

SIMPLIFIED PRODUCT IDENTIFICATION

These two product lines, designed by the DuPuis Group, demonstrate how brand blocking can be created. The key for any strong brand block is to make it easy for consumers to shop once they have involved themselves with the brand.

Brand Blocking

Brand blocking refers to the cumulative effect achieved when a section of a shelf set is clearly dominated by a particular brand through the effective use of well-branded packaging. More than ever, in this context, branding is not just the logo on the pack but, rather, the visual fingerprint the whole group of packages makes on shelf.

Big brands in certain categories seem to own a shelf. Often this is driven by a color that causes consumers to immedi-ately recognize the brand. In the freezer case, you will encounter the Popsicle yellow door. In the breakfast/snack aisle, you will find the blue wall of Pop-Tarts.

One extension of brand blocking is sometimes referred to as billboarding, the rhythmic or patterned appearance that occurs when multiple product facings work together to form a larger impression. Billboarding can be engaging, but as a technique it sometimes feels like a forced effort to be clever at the expense of optimal product shopability.

It is critical for large products lines to have a careful balance intended to attract the consumer. Brand blocking should draw them in with bold colors or large blocks of color, but at the same time, it must be easy to shop. This requires careful consideration in creating an intuitive shopping system. A number of design devices help: color, shape, fonts, photography, and so on. It's essential to give flavors a clear difference close up but a group feel at a distance.

Shopability: **MAKING** Vast Product Lines **EASY** to Navigate

If finding what they want within your client's brand's offerings makes consumers rub their eyes in confusion, you have a shopability problem. For instance, one brand of pasta sauce with thirty-seven flavors is simply too hard to navigate. Often a consumer will buy another brand rather than sort it out. However, the situation is different when flavors are segmented based on clear criteria, such as organic versus not organic, meaty versus meatless, or perhaps based on significant price breaks, like budget versus gourmet blends. Consumers can locate a group and then locate their flavor. If a product line is segmented in a way that is irrelevant to consumers, they'll probably move on to the store brand that is easier to understand and probably cheaper, too.

Assuming a typical line of products that isn't unnecessarily wide, shopability can be easily achieved through consistent design architecture. With clear, legible typography and a judicious use of color and/or imagery, a package design system can provide quick, relevant distinctions.

Enrich the Shelf Life

Products and packaging living a risk-averse shelf life are playing it safe. As a rule, however, this approach leads to flat results and additional vulnerability to defeat. The edgier or more aggressive players are arguably taking more chances, but they know that with good planning and smart changes, greater riches are there for the taking. Designers need to encourage smart risk taking by their clients in order to avoid products being lumped in as parity products. Standing out on the shelf over time requires revitalization of package designs.

How We See

This is the order in which humans see:
1. Color
2. Shape
3. Photography
4. Words

Designers and clients must understand this sequence and apply it to the way consumers will see their product packaging.

Brand Segmentation

The following elements can be used to extend a product line:

- Color
- Linking elements
- Graphic architecture
- Photography
- Typography
- Brand hierarchy

A careful balance needs to be achieved when developing brand blocking and a clear concise shopping system. Visual architecture needs to take into account product flavors and forms. Both the Sargento cheeses and the Quaker breakfast offerings, designed by DuPuis, use color, linking elements, and photography to boost shopability.

Creating Effective SHOPPING SYSTEMS

Ending consumer confusion, especially when they are shopping brands with a large number of flavor, style, or price-point options, is a challenge for designers and marketers. However, there are a number of ways to help ensure a more effective shopping experience. When designing for increased shopability, the following milestones must be accomplished:

- Create a billboard effect to draw consumers to the brand
- Provide clear differentiation in varieties
- Show the benefits and appeal of the product
- Hierarchically organize competing elements and imagery
- Spotlight innovations and features
- Connect emotionally with buyers
- Design for flexibility and expansion of the line

Packaging for the Nivea product range, by Just Blue Design, has a consistent structural shape, but uses color as a means to create distinctions between product varieties. While Caffè Artigiano coffees by Subplot Design uses photography to differentiate.

Case Study | Knobbly-Carrot

The Knobbly-Carrot Organic Food Company, a soup manufacturer, came to designers Taxi Studio with two major problems: declining sales and product confusion. Consumers assumed that because of the company's name, carrots were an ingredient in all products, which wasn't true. The Knobbly Company refused to change their name. So the packaging was radically redesigned with veggie paintings and the brand renamed Knobbly-Carrot Family—Masters of Organic Foods. The new packs brought the brand's simmering sales to a boil, increasing distribution and introducing the Knobbly-Carrot to a wider circle of shoppers.

Breaking Through the **BURST BARRIER**

"NEW & IMPROVED!" "NEW LOOK, SAME GREAT TASTE!" "NOW EVEN BETTER!" "MAXIMUM STRENGTH!" "25 PERCENT MORE FREE!" "NO SUGAR ADDED!" These are but a few of the messages designers are regularly asked to feature on a package. *Burst, violator,* and *snipe* are fairly synonymous terms for any graphic vehicle meant to violate a layout for the sake of shouting a message. They are intentionally disruptive, to some degree, and should be judiciously utilized to announce truly new news that is often of a temporary nature. If you have children, you know that shouting all the time creates deafness and a chronic decline in attention, so don't beat up your consumer with bursts.

However, when a message is more permanent and helpful in the identification of a segment within your line, such as "LOW-FAT" on a yogurt or "WITH VITAMIN E" on a cosmetic or beauty product, it is better to integrate the message than to violate the layout. Integrated messages can still grab attention but have a more involved, harmonious role in the layout.

Product benefits and nutritional information are becoming more important to consumers. Within Lightlife, DuPuis integrated this information in the front PDP, and used it to convey the personality of the brand.

With the rise in nutritional awareness, informational elements are often used on the primary display panel (PDP). Dole's Wildly Nutritious line, created by DuPuis, presents an antioxidant message on one pack and a healthy heart message on the other.

"New" is used to tell consumers of new products within a line and may appear on the package for the first six months only. The prominence and use of "new" on packages has become so common it's less effective than it used to be. In the clutter and proliferation of these bursts, consumers have learned to tune them out.

Informing the Consumer:
SPECIAL LABELING

Governments and other regulating bodies in various countries all over the globe have set standards for consumer information and safety. What this means to designers is working within the requirements, while still creating a compelling on-brand package. It's important to understand and consider these legalities that must be incorporated right from the start of the design process.

What Information?

The kinds of labeling requirements imposed on a package have to do with the type of product it is, its distribution and retailing needs, and the laws of the country it will be sold in. These can include nutritional information on food items, warnings on chemicals and potentially hazardous materials, shipping information including the fragile nature of the item, and stocking system codes.

Everything from how to eat a balanced diet to a warning about possible child suffocation can restrict the aesthetics of a design. Waiting until the end of the design process, and being faced with cramming in an encyclopedia's worth of minute type on the package, is not going

to work. Even simple information, like bulk weight, country of origin, exact ingredients or materials, and recycling configurations, can eat up precious space.

Where is the Information?

The front primary display panel (PDP) is predominantly a branding and sales tool, while the back panel will typically provide consumer information details. Things like the U.S. Government's NLEA Nutrition Facts Chart, ingredients list, directions for use, warnings and precautions, and the UPC scan code will usually appear here. If the package has side panels, there is obviously more space for additional information, perhaps recipes or additional product shots. If the package has a top and bottom, this provides space for an additional PDP for alternative shelf stocking ability, so that the product can appear either horizontally or vertically on a shelf.

Nesquick by Bloom Design is an example of how designers in the UK must integrate required nutritional information.

U.S. Nutritional Labeling Education Act (NLEA) Facts Chart

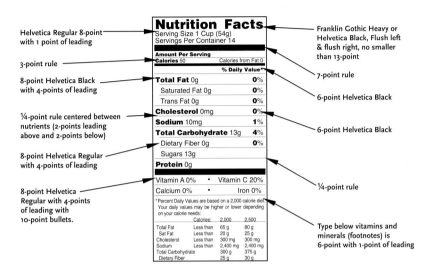

Helvetica Regular 8-point with 1 point of leading

3-point rule

8-point Helvetica Black with 4-points of leading

¼-point rule centered between nutrients (2-points leading above and 2-points below)

8-point Helvetica Regular with 4-points of leading

8-point Helvetica Regular with 4-points of leading with 10-point bullets.

Franklin Gothic Heavy or Helvetica Black, Flush left & flush right, no smaller than 13-point

7-point rule

6-point Helvetica Black

6-point Helvetica Black

¼-point rule

Type below vitamins and minerals (footnotes) is 6-point with 1-point of leading

Nutrition Facts
Serving Size 1 Cup (54g)
Servings Per Container 14

Amount Per Serving
Calories 50   Calories from Fat 0

% Daily Value*

Total Fat 0g	**0**%
Saturated Fat 0g	**0**%
Trans Fat 0g	**0**%
Cholesterol 0mg	**0**%
Sodium 10mg	**1**%
Total Carbohydrate 13g	**4**%
Dietary Fiber 0g	**0**%
Sugars 13g	
Protein 0g	

Vitamin A 0%	•	Vitamin C 20%
Calcium 0%	•	Iron 0%

*Percent Daily Values are based on a 2,000 calorie diet. Your daily values may be higher or lower depending on your calorie needs:

		Calories:	2,000	2,500
Total Fat	Less than		65 g	80 g
Sat Fat	Less than		20 g	25 g
Cholesterol	Less than		300 mg	300 mg
Sodium	Less than		2,400 mg	2,400 mg
Total Carbohydrate			300 g	375 g
Dietary Fiber			25 g	30 g

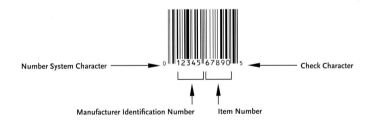

Number System Character

0 12345 67890 5

Check Character

Manufacturer Identification Number   Item Number

Anatomy of a UPC (Universal Product Code)

A UPC code is a series of bars and numerals that get scanned with infrared light, and are used for tracking, stocking, and pricing of products throughout the world.

- **Number System Character**
  The first code of the UPC is assigned by the Uniform Code Council and indicates the number system that is to follow.

- **Manufacturer Identification Number**
  The unique 5-digit number also assigned by the Uniform Code Council

- **Item Number**
  The 5-digit number assigned and controlled by the product manufacturer/owner

- **Check Character**
  The last number of the UPC is used to verify the accuracy of the entire UPC.

Packaging Regulations

What you can say and not say on-pack is often closely governed by local, state, and federal guidelines. In addition, a plethora of boards, institutes, and acts issue certifications that ensure products meet certain qualifications. Among these many governing bodies and acts are:

- Food and Drug Administration (FDA): health and nutritional claims
- Nutritional Labeling Education Act (NLEA): standardized nutrition labeling and formatting criteria
- Federal Trade Commission (FTC): environmental and advertising claims
- Fair Packaging and Labeling Act (FPLA): net content and origin/manufacturer disclosures
- National Conference on Weights and Measures (NCWM): protects equity in the marketplace
- Environmental Protection Agency (EPA): develops and enforces environmental regulations
- Department of Commerce, National Institute of Standards and Technology (NIST): promotes measurement standards
- National trade and industry associations
- International government organizations

Informing the Consumer:
SIDE AND BACK PANELS

Packaging design is a three-dimensional experience. After the PDP is approved and line extension systems are in development, the back and side panels then need to be created. All too often this area is left until the end of a project, and not given the strategic thinking necessary for achieving maximum results. Designers need to think of packaging from a holistic point of view, and even though it may not be discussed at the onset of a job, its function and purpose need to be kept in mind. The back panel and other sides of a package can and do serve in completing a sale. They can extend the story of the brand and product, allowing consumers to experience the brand further if they choose. For new consumers, these panels can be the closer when comparing products. These panels are also places for nutritional information, additional product benefits, specifications, and legal requirements.

Multiple Uses
The strategy behind these various package panels is dependent on consumer involvement within a category. Healthy and organic consumers seek information and spend a longer time with a product in a grocery setting before purchases. Cereal boxes see usage after the sale by providing games and information that invites kids to experience the brand each time they eat the product. Consumer goods use these panels to show how to use the product or call out special features that may sway consumers at purchase.

Multiple Languages
More and more marketers are considering the use of multiple languages on packages. Economics of scale make it a smart move to create packages that work for entire regions of the globe (e.g. all of North and South America, thus requiring English, Spanish, and French). More than that, multilingual packages reach out to consumer groups in their own languages, attracting new buyers. Some countries/areas require bilingual packaging by law (e.g. Quebec, Canada). However, multiple languages do present a design challenge. Copyfitting massive amounts of text can clutter the package, and risk making it appeal to no one instead of everyone.

The back panel label for Spot Shot, designed by DuPuis, provides a wealth of information for consumers, including: product features, endorsements, directions for use, warnings, and the UPC scan code.

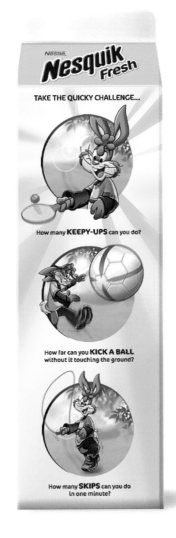

Nestlé has developed its own means of providing consumers with more information about nutrition and well-being via their Nutritional Compass. On each of its products, Nestlé supplies "It's Good to Know" details about some aspect of the product contained within. In the case of Dark Raisinets, designed by DuPuis, the Nutritional Compass talks about the antioxidant qualities of raisins and chocolate. Note that the text is also bilingual. For Nesquick, by Bloom, there is information about the vitamins found in milk.

Package Production:
LOOKING BACK and LOOKING AHEAD

An Interview with Bob Squibb, *Quality Assurance Ambassador, Schawk, Inc., Stamford, CT*

Q. *What is your role at Schawk, Inc.?*
A. I am a print management consultant and quality control expert for Schawk, the world's largest separator and brand imaging provider. I have over 30 years of experience in the separation and printing industry.

Q. *What innovations have changed the role of packaging most over recent years, and how?*
A. There have been huge advances in prepress and printing technologies. The most amazing improvements have been in high-speed web flexographic printing. With the development of digital polymer plates, flexography is able to handle projects it's never been able to before. Flexo can hold ever-improving line quality and deliver amazing color contrast; it often can be mistaken for offset or gravure. Of course, you have to properly prepare the separations for flexo to get the best results.

Q. *What common mistakes do you see being made that hurt the production of great packaging?*
A. The biggest mistake I see is clients cutting corners to save time. Many just don't give themselves or us enough time to do things right. You need enough time for proofreading and making revisions and quality separations.

Another big mistake is clients not telling the designer what printing method is going to be used on a given job. You can't design it properly unless you know what print medium will be used for reproduction. You should hold preproduction meetings early to troubleshoot the design.

Q. *What can design firms do differently to get the most out of current print production technologies?*
A. They can involve the separator in the design process and consult with us, even before design presentations to clients or official pre-pro meetings. If a designer comes up with designs that can't be reproduced properly, it makes the designer look bad to the client and only disappoints. Designers need to manage client expectations before everyone gets married to a design. Once it's sold to a client, the designer looks foolish if it ultimately can't be printed.

Q. *What are your clients' greatest needs that you fulfill?*
A. Quality assurance—maintaining the integrity of the design throughout the printing process, all over the world. The brands we serve demand consistency globally, and that's no easy task.

Q. *What do you see as the biggest challenge for brand manufacturers?*
A. The entire packaging industry is becoming more educated about and sensitive to environmental issues. Sustainability is a very big factor. Producing less waste and getting rid of it is a big challenge with more and more people on the planet. We need to recycle and reuse. It's a tough job for designers and their clients to meet these changing demands, but corporations need to address the public's growing outcry for greener processes.

Q. What do you see as the biggest challenge for separators?

A. Shorter turnaround times. There is just no more time left to cut out. If we are continually asked to produce things in less time, then clients need to be satisfied with lesser results.

Q. How do you see the printing and separation industry changing in the next five years?

A. Packaging has a direct link to environmental concerns. Increasingly, consumers will be looking to reduce waste and will frown more and more on excessive packaging. This will create the need for different kinds of packaging, for new, more efficient, or cleaner-to-produce materials, and less of them. I don't know how it's going to change exactly; I only know it must.

Case Study

The process of creating Dark Raisinets, a new, more sophisticated incarnation of the classic Nestlé treat, revealed untapped opportunities within the original flavor line-up. After establishing a new packaging architecture, including the addition of a heath message captured in a green banner graphic, Dark Raisinets became more relevant and visually enticing to existing and new consumers who want sweet favorites as well as a healthy lifestyle.

How to Read a **DIELINE**

The digital document that contains a precise drawing indicating the shape and structural specifications of a package is known as a *dieline*. Due to the vast array of packaging formats and media, all dieline or template standards cannot be addressed in singular terms. However, these general features and issues should be identified when reading a dieline.

Scores, Cuts, and Perforations

There is a reason why each line in a dieline is solid (cut edge or trim), dashed (often used for folds or scores), or occasionally broken with short gaps (perforations or kiss-cuts). It is also common to find different colors of linework used to delineate boundaries for trim, bleed (a small area beyond the die to which color must extend to allow for slight cut misalignment), and live area (a cautionary zone in which all critical information and visuals must be kept within to ensure visibility).

Glue Areas or No-Print Zones

Usually called out in supplemental notes from the manufacturer, certain areas are often kept clear of inks and coatings for proper glue adhesion or for post-production imprinting of best-before dates or lot numbers. Flexible packaging may also have no-ink or no-live-art requirements in fin-seal and heat-crimping regions.

UPC Area

The position of a UPC (or similar) code is often flexible but may be indicated in the dieline to ensure it is placed at the correct angle or size for optimal reproduction and scanability.

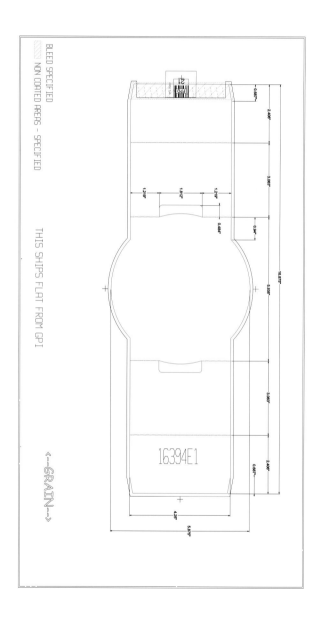

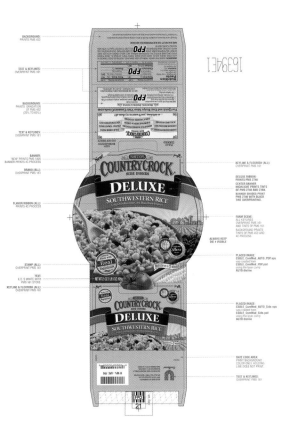

Panel Orientation and/or Press Direction

Cartons or paperboard packages with multiple panels or facets may require that art be prepared facing certain directions or with a certain relationship to one another. For instance, many food companies establish a standard that the nutritional panel is always oriented on the immediate leftward panel from the primary display panel (PDP). Print side and press direction may also be called out to prevent inadvertent flipping of a die and as a reminder for numerous prepress considerations.

Eye Marks and Eye Channels or Lanes

In the case of flexible packaging on film such as bags, one or two small black (or high-contrast color) marks measuring approximately $1/4 \times 5/8$ inch (6 × 16 mm) are positioned along a specific edge, and the space between them must be kept clear. This open space is the eye channel and is used by a mechanical eye that watches for the eye mark as the film passes by for cutting indication.

Other Miscellaneous Markings

Dimensions should always be used to verify the scale of a dieline at first use and will serve to confirm actual size throughout the package's development. Many other dieline specs may be present that are not easily understood. Separating such elements onto different layers is sensible, but be sure not to discard them altogether because they are there for a reason and may be important to another process.

Need Modifications?

Dielines should be altered only with the agreed consent of the printer, as they usually represent an existing die tool that will have to be altered as well. These changes can be costly and can produce crippling problems later if done without authorization. It is best to leave any modifications to the manufacturer who provided them.

QUALITY CONTROL of Production Art/Finished File

Whether the pre-pro meeting is with a large group of vendors for a complex packaging program or an internal assessment on smaller jobs, it is helpful to have a checklist for review of main points that ensure a clean release of artwork. In general, it is smart to review finished files in the following areas:

- **Dielines**—Verify as accurate and implemented correctly. Common mistakes:
- Art built on an inverted (flipped) dieline
- Art oriented incorrectly on panels (rotation, adjacency, etc)
- Bleeds and no-ink areas (often for best-before date coding) not accounted for
- Eye channels (flexible packaging) not kept clear or eye mark contrast too low
- Seals (bags) and/or overlaps (can labels) not allowed for
- Packs trimmed with single-knife cuts (shared edges) not built to do so. What bleeds off one edge must carry over to the other or be framed in a solid.

- **Print Process**—Art is crafted appropriately for given process and within spec. Common mistakes:
- Type and other small elements built with unrealistic color builds or too small/fine. Registering two or more screened colors to build complex colors is often problematic on press, especially in flexographic printing. Minimum type sizes should be observed; 6-point is most common but can be smaller in better processes or larger as a knock-out or in lower-end printing processes.
- Excessive number of inks specified in the art. Ink count is limited by press configuration and/or allocated budget.
- Gradations, vignettes, or fine tints exceed press capabilities; especially in flexographic printing, Minimum dot requirements and analox ratings play a pivotal role in dictating these tolerances.

- **Image quality**—Verify sufficient resolution, correct color space, usage rights obtained, etc. Common mistakes:
- Images linked as RGB rather than CMYK or as multichannel spot color images

- Low-resolution images that will not sufficiently support the process. The standard 300 dpi is acceptable, but less can work depending on the application.
- Image rights missing or outdated. Unauthorized image duplication is a huge problem and is being dealt with aggressively by those whose rights are infringed. Be sure you have the correct usage rights and/or licensing to print every image.

- **Content quality control**—A good rule of thumb is to have three individuals from different disciplines—for example, designer, project manager, and technical proofreader—proof the content for accuracy. Common mistakes:
- Misspelling: Spellcheck helps, but proprietary vernacular often requires special attention.
- Poor use of language. Copy can be spelled right and properly punctuated but still say the wrong thing or be misleading.
- Missing elements. In the digital world, design elements can drop off a layout for many reasons between the design and production stages. Designers often look to see if what we see is right but forget to look for what we do not see.

- **Regulatory and legal details**—Examples: ® versus ™, kosher symbols (which one?), © and corporate signoffs, certification symbols (used properly?), UPCs (scale limitations, color use, rotation versus press direction, truncation okay?), recycling symbols, NLEA and net weight regulations (minimum type sizes per package size and keep-clear areas, etc.)

- **Annotations**—Prepress notes to the separator, color assignments, FPO indications, special treatment notes, and digital file meta data all should be clear. Common mistakes:
- Vague or overly complex annotations that can easily confuse
- Poorly placed callouts that make content proofing difficult
- Lack of version documentation and clear approval status
- Conflicting color assignments via errors in callouts or multiple color swatches for one color
- Outdated callouts from legacy/repurposed art that have not been retrofitted for a new line extension

---

STRATEGIC BRAND DESIGN

Quality Control Checklist

DU PUIS

- [ ] Before Pre-Pro Meeting
  Canon Print out
  with Client sign-off
- [ ] After Production
  Canon Print out
  with Client sign-off
- [ ] After Pre-Press
  Canon Print out
- [ ] Final with proof
  Kodak, Waterproof, etc
  Need Client signoff to go to sep
- [ ] Other:

PLEASE CHECK CAREFULLY ALONG WITH THE FOLLOWING LIST.

Columns: Q.C. Specialist, Project Manager, Creative Director, Designer

• 3 Signatures minimum needed before going to the next stage

Q.C. Specialist	Project Manager	Creative Director	Designer		
[ ]	[ ]	[ ]	[ ]	**Product names**	spelling, TM, registrations, consistency of usage
[ ]	[ ]	[ ]	[ ]	**Spelling**	names, titles, affiliations
[ ]	[ ]	[ ]	[ ]	**Address**	numbers, locations, and telephone/fax numbers
[ ]	[ ]	[ ]	[ ]	**Legal information**	©, ®, TM, corporate credits and consistency of usage
[ ]	[ ]	[ ]	[ ]	**Bleed**	Check all areas that need bleed.
[ ]	[ ]	[ ]	[ ]	**Page numbers**	sequence, continuations, position
[ ]	[ ]	[ ]	[ ]	**Sizes**	Check all dimensions, R&L margins, centering, alignment.
[ ]	[ ]	[ ]	[ ]	**Color**	How many color will be used? 4 color process, Spot color(s) Have all the colors not used been deleted from the digital file? Color approved by client with Canon, PMS swatches, Patch or Press-Match?
[ ]	[ ]	[ ]	[ ]	**Die cutting or punching**	Does die cut fit? Do holes clear copy? Supplied with digital file, or just dimension?
[ ]	[ ]	[ ]	[ ]	**Revisions**	Have you checked each revision against prior specs?
[ ]	[ ]	[ ]	[ ]	**Color call-out** (if needed)	Have you marked all keyline deletions, reverses, screens, dropouts behind colors or type?
[ ]	[ ]	[ ]	[ ]	**Time Frame**	Check the deadline again. Do we have enough pre-press time?
[ ]	[ ]	[ ]	[ ]	**Are File Name/ Date & Time / Version indicated on print out?**	

1. SIGNATURE DATE

2. SIGNATURE DATE

3. SIGNATURE DATE

4. SIGNATURE DATE

COMMENTS

_____

_____

_____

_____

BE BOLD

BE CREATIVE

BE A LEADER

www.dupuisgroup.com

Printing **PROCESSES**

Future Printing Processes

Looking ahead, new printing methods will likely be focusing on biofriendly processes, increased speed with equal or better quality, and more digital intervention. In addition, high-tech printing technologies in modern manufacturing processes may bring revolutionary track ing and tamper evidence/authentication innovations to packaged product niches. Innovative inks that contain electrostatic properties and the ability to store encrypted manufacturing data and codes, sometimes virtually undetectable to the eye, are being tested and developed. These innovations could affect high-security and high price point product niches like pharmaceuticals, and all products that have a great deal to lose from tampering or piracy.

Beyond specific printing processes are supplemental techniques, such as thermoform or in-the-round shrinkpack film, that afford greater flexibility in both the form and function of packaging. The field is exciting, and designers must keep up with new printing technologies in order to leverage these advances for their clients.

OFFSET LITHOGRAPHY

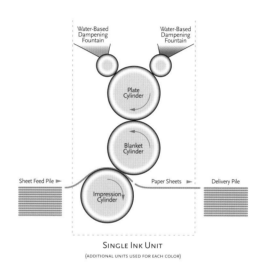

SINGLE INK UNIT
(ADDITIONAL UNITS USED FOR EACH COLOR)

ROTOGRAVURE

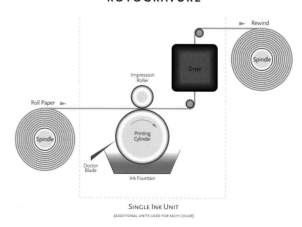

SINGLE INK UNIT
(ADDITIONAL UNITS USED FOR EACH COLOR)

SCREEN PRINTING

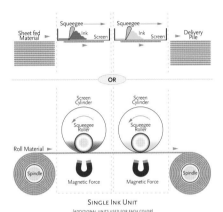

Squeegee   Squeegee

Sheet fed Material   Ink   Screen   Ink   Screen   Delivery Pile

OR

Screen Cylinder   Screen Cylinder

Squeegee Roller   Squeegee Roller

Roll Material

Spindle   Magnetic Force   Magnetic Force   Spindle

SINGLE INK UNIT
(ADDITIONAL UNITS USED FOR EACH COLOR)

FLEXOGRAPHY

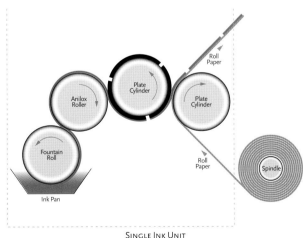

Roll Paper

Plate Cylinder

Anilox Roller   Plate Cylinder

Fountain Roll

Roll Paper   Spindle

Ink Pan

SINGLE INK UNIT
(ADDITIONAL UNITS USED FOR EACH COLOR)

Global Printing Processes for Packaging

- **Flexography**—Flexible polymer plates, wide ink capabilities, great for variety of printing surfaces. Huge advances in last few years have made flexo a player where only offset litho and gravure could have sufficed before.
- **Offset lithography**—Great image quality and control, fairly easy plate-making, sheet or roll fed
- **Rotogravure**—Engraved copper cylinders, rotary press, usually roll-fed, great ink density range, good for long runs
- **Silkscreen**—Framed stencil-type process, great for textiles and hardware but relatively low image detail capability
- **Digital printing**—Virtually the same as offset lithography but without physical plate production and smaller in format and slower; plates are digital imagers that can be changed per impression and modified easily. Not used widely for packaging yet but shows growing promise in yielding short-run, variable data options that require little or no warehousing and are attractive in a world that wants more new news faster and faster.

PROOFING and Press CHECKS

One of the greater printing challenges for designers that came with the digital revolution is within the proofing process. Prior to digital plate-making (DTP/CTP), film negatives were produced for each color separation and used to make the proof, typically a Matchprint or a Chromalin, and again later for the making of plates used on the presses. Provided these two steps were managed and calibrated correctly, you had a largely apples-to-apples comparison from proof to print. When film was replaced by digital postscript files, finding new, cost-effective ways to produce an accurate proof seemed virtually impossible.

Proofing Options

Today, several options exist that have become commonly accepted, much like the Matchprint of yesteryear, but designers and their printing partners still struggle to produce reliable simulations of what will happen on press. The technologies used to simulate dot gain, spread, UCR/GCR, and so on have come a long way, but there is still a need for better spot color representation. Many proofing systems do not accurately show dot but are sometimes continuous-tone simulations. Good old-fashioned ink draw-downs and color chips are still the gold standards.

Ink Innovations

Another big curve ball, yet opportunity, is the emergence of new ink technologies such as Pantone's Hexachrome, which is the standard four-color process (CMYK) plus orange and green for greater color range, and Opaltone, which is CMYK plus red, green, and blue inks. These proprietary ink systems provide big color-range and ink density benefits but also require custom software, proofing, and separation techniques that can add complexity, a steep learning curve, and in some cases additional expense.

Press Checks

Once on press, having accurate proofs on hand becomes critical to having a target and goal for color. Those proofs are usually broadly routed, reviewed, and approved by clients who will not be press-side, so making sure the printed job looks like the proofs is vital in order to satisfy expectations.

It's ideal to have an experienced representative from not only the printer (for example, the pressman or printing sales representative) but also the client and design firm at press side. With all parties present, the compromises that often must be made on press can either be agreed on and approved or immediately rejected—and the run stopped.

When considering options at press side that affect the finished result, it is important that the real end results be kept in mind. Ultimately, it's not whether you matched a proof or not but, rather, what the consumer will actually find on the shelf. Brand stewardship never stops, even when ink hits paper. Color equities, projected value—it all comes down to the final print production. It is at this critical point that decisions made regarding substrate quality, ink usage, print process selection, not to mention the printer choice in itself, can make or break success in the consumer's eyes. Again, don't fumble on the 1-yard line.

mexican
beef fajita
wrap

mild salsa & avocado dip

munch
yumm

Price $5.95

Use by

wraps are chock full
ingredients
p in a tasty tortilla.

yumm munch

new flavour yumm

munch
money

turn me over
to open

Fresh

munch

cheese,
tomato
& onion

sweet pickles

Vegie
friendly

munch
yumm

Use by: 18/10/08   Price: $4.95

Case Study

Australia's oldest and leading convenience retailer, 7-Eleven, recognized the need to present
a more compelling and differentiated ready-to-
eat meal offering to update their increasingly
tired quickie-mart image and drive more traffic
and sales. A new brand, called *munch*, was
created with high expectations: to become part
of the customers' lunchtime routine, generate
category sales growth by 10 percent every year,
shift the 7-Eleven brand perception, and create
a new destination brand. Future Brand designed
the *munch* packaging to convey freshness, convenience, and fun; as a result, sandwich sales
have increased by 48 percent, fruit salads by 72
percent, and drinks by 50 percent.

chocky milk
500mL

real
cocoa

munch
yumm

totally
iced coffee
500mL

Cool
coffee
hit

munch
yumm

orange juice
500mL

munch

DESIGN'S REAL WORLD
RETURN ON INVESTMENT

Case studies in package design excellence

Designing a Deeper
CUSTOMER CONNECTION

With stores throughout England, Waitrose combines the convenience of a supermarket with the expertise and service of a specialty shop. Distinctly upmarket and ethically aware, Waitrose is renowned for the unparalleled quality, traceability, and freshness of its natural and organic meats, produce, and specialty foods.

For fifteen years, Turner Duckworth has designed Waitrose's own-brand products to play a highly visible and integral role in delivering a unique brand and in-store experience.

The Waitrose own-brands—from canned vegetables to cookies to pet food to sparkling juices—help provide validation and encouragement for its customers' lifestyles and healthy eating choices. Their prominence and ubiquity on-shelf give the brands the power to individually and collectively express Waitrose's unique spirit, ethos, and authenticity.

The customer connection built by its own brands has evolved into a powerful emotional bond that fosters enduring loyalty and enhances the overall Waitrose promise.

Turner Duckworth's designs reflect Waitrose's subtle and sophisticated aesthetic by emphasizing ingredients, provenance, and flavor. No clutter, no violators, no loud graphics—just delicious food presented beautifully with understated elegance, originality, style, and wit.

Turner Duckworth's designs make shopping easier, more pleasurable, and more informative for Waitrose customers. And once they're in homes, Waitrose's own-brand products continue to deliver on their promise by making it easy to select, prepare, and serve wholesome, natural, and delicious meals every day.

OPEN HERE

OPEN HERE

Waitrose GRISSINI **BREADSTICKS**
PLAIN

BAKED IN ITALY

Waitrose *Torinesi* **BREADSTICKS**
with Extra Virgin Olive Oil

BAKED IN ITALY

Waitrose
FRENCH SUNFLOWER HONEY

Waitrose
ACACIA HONEY

Waitrose
ITALIAN CHESTNUT HONEY

Waitrose
AUSTRALIAN
BLOSSOM HONEY

Waitrose
ORANGE BLOSSOM HONEY

Brand Identity for a **NEW PRODUCT LINE** of Paints and Varnishes

The client, the Colibri Group, based in St. Petersburg, Russia, approached Asgard after acquiring a paint and varnish factory. The factory's products were being sold under generic names; there were no graphic identifiers for the products or for the factory, let alone any visual system; the packaging (metal cans) bore nondescript paper labels. The main goals were to set the client's products apart from competing products, to create a new brand that would be easily identifiable, and to help the products win shelf space.

At the time the client set out to create a new brand, the market was saturated, but the look of the products available in the determined price range did not meet customers' expectations and perceptions of packaging design, which have changed during the last decade. Even in this entirely practical field, consumers have become much more demanding in terms of both product quality and product visual communications. Most domestic products in this category, however, still looked outdated.

The consumers were identified as people of low and middle incomes who

VOICE OF SUCCESS

"Thanks to the successful design of the packaging, we saved a significant portion of the company's advertising budget during the launch stage of the new product line."

DANIIL PETROV
Marketing Director,
First Paints & Varnishes Factory

"Today production capacity reaches 2,000 tons (1814.4 metric tons) of paints, varnishes, and other construction materials per month."

ILYA GRIGORYEV
Public Relations Officer,
First Paints & Varnishes Factory

renovate their homes themselves or are keen do-it-yourselfers as well as small crews of builders and interior decorators who work for private clients. The consumers are in their late twenties to late fifties, with a wide range of cultural, work, and psychological profiles.

The product line was positioned as medium-priced, to be retailed both by big DIY stores and small shops. It included four types of products: oil-based paints, water-based paints, enamels, and varnishes. The products are sold in 1-quart (0.95 L), 2.5-gallon (9.5 L), and 5-gallon (19 L) metal cans and very well-recieved by consumers.

STARTING A REVOLUTION, One Potato Peeler at a Time

When Smart Design began its collaboration with OXO in 1990, kitchen gadgets were pretty much limited to $1.99 (£1) vegetable peelers and other undifferentiated, price-driven products. With Good Grips, Smart Design and OXO revolutionized the market by creating high-quality tools that addressed the needs of the widest range of people possible.

Great Design Identity

OXO asked Smart Design to develop a brand identity and packaging system to be used with the full line of OXO products. Like the products, the identity had to be simple and straightforward. It had to communicate the product's benefits to the consumer, be easy to display, and encourage consumers to touch and feel the product.

Everyone Gets It

The black, white, and red elements of the packaging allow clear communication to the consumer and provide a platform that shows off the product. Encouraging touching and handling of the products, the packaging advocates the philosophy of universal design—these products are good for everybody. The packaging system is adaptable, giving consistency to the company's entire line of products. As the years go by, the branding system can be flexible but remains reliable in the consumer's eye, firmly entrenching OXO as the go-to housewares brand.

OPEN HERE

"OXO's minimal packaging exposes the handles, allowing consumers to touch and squeeze the merchandise before purchasing it and to learn for themselves how comfortably the product fits in their hand."

DAVID STOWELL
CEO/Founder,
Smart Design

"We needed customers to stop and think, 'That's something different.' The more the product itself can communicate visually, the less packaging is needed."

SAM FARBER
Founder,
OXO

When Creative Direction and Packaging Architecture Work **HAND IN HAND**

When the heads of men's product design and merchandising felt existing packaging for Old Navy basics, like underwear and T-shirts, was not in line with the direction of upcoming product and did not distinguish itself from the competition, they challenged packaging design to elevate the product with a new structure and creative voice.

Sales of these basics, although a staple of the Old Navy business, were essentially flat. A reinvention and elevation of the brand packaging could potentially reintroduce customers to the product and reinforce brand messaging while raising perceived value and allowing a higher price point without a negative impact on units sold.

A Surplus of Imagination

At task was to clarify the voice of men's and boys' Old Navy basics and raise the product to a higher level in the marketplace. To achieve this, art director Jason Rosenberg set out to design entirely new creative that would work hand in hand with a new packaging architecture.

OPEN HERE

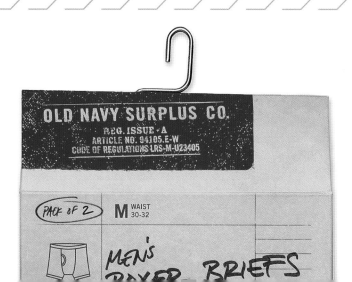

OLD NAVY SURPLUS CO.
REG. ISSUE - A
ARTICLE NO. 94105.E-W
CODE OF REGULATIONS-LRS-M-U23405

PACK OF 2 M WAIST 30-32

MEN'S
BOXER BRIEFS

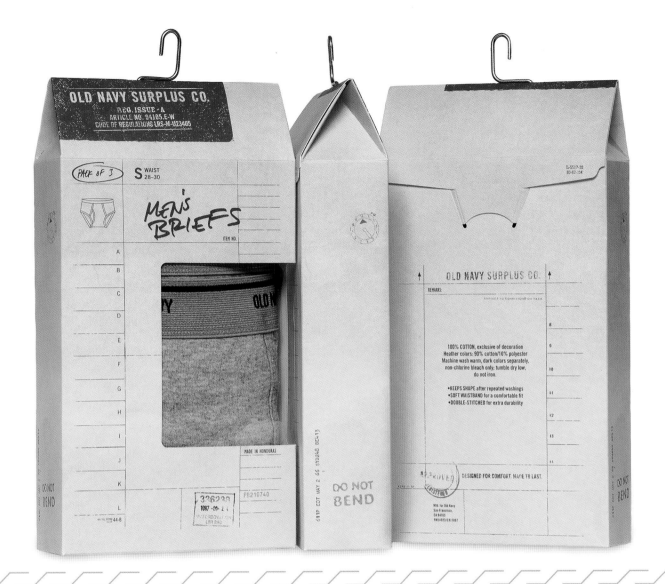

Distinctive design, materials, and packaging structure helped establish a core look and strong shelf recognition with Old Navy's spirit and authenticity throughout the line.

157

Signed, Sealed, Delivered

To accomplish these goals, an overall concept of surplus was developed. Rosenberg sought to graphically establish the imagery of an everyday business communiqué between the Old Navy Surplus Company and its customer.

Designing the packages with an interoffice aesthetic, Rosenberg utilized die cuts from mailing envelopes and manila folders. He created a kraft paper backdrop for a memo-like grid system that remains consistent throughout all of the packaging variations. Actual handwriting was used to call out the product category with bureaucratic stamp motifs placed throughout. Employing innovative digital production and printing techniques, a realistic look was achieved—as if the package had just been written on and freshly delivered from the office mailroom.

"Everything in the office environment was explored," says Rosenberg, "from vintage ledgers to paper clips to wax seals. Finding ways to capture these elements in the packaging was an exciting challenge." Materials were chosen that would further establish this aesthetic— for example, printing on uncoated paper stock and the string-tie button closure on the boxer gift box. The men's shoebox features creative use of a high-gloss spot varnish; it looks like packing tape and Scotch tape hold the box together. The development of an antiqued metal hook as an alternative to the normal plastic hook drove the theme home.

Having a strong and cohesive brand packaging system in-store speaks volumes to the Old Navy customer but it appears to be driving sales results as well. With the new package design launched in fall 2007, results have already been positive.

Supply and Demand

According to senior men's merchandiser Brain Richardson, "Old Navy's new basic underwear and sock packaging has played a key role in growing the business by elevating the product, allowing us to drive a higher retail price. This has differentiated us from our competitors. It makes the shopping experience easier and visual presentation more attractive, resulting in growth in the business from a 12 percent AUR (average unit retail price) increase and 28 percent higher gross margin. Since our customer has not been sensitive to the higher ticketed price, we've been able to be more profitable today."

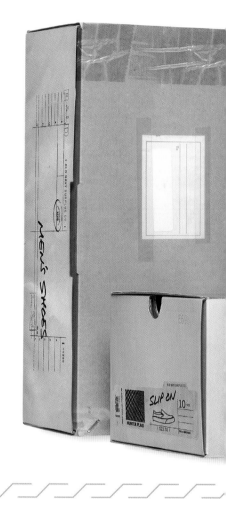

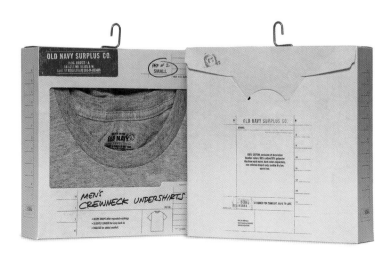

A New **PREMIUM TEA BRAND** is Ready to Indulge Hotels and Restaurants

Gebrueder Wollenhaupt is a major German tea company that was established in 1881 and based in Hamburg. The brand name Wollenhaupt in Germany stands for premium tea pleasure and indulgence, with the highest standards of quality and service.

Targeting New Markets

To gain further market shares in the fast-growing catering market, Wollenhaupt wanted to introduce a new tea brand to three- and four-star hotels, restaurants, and upscale cafés. Furthermore, with the help of the new brand, Wollenhaupt wanted to exploit new markets via new sales channels such as independent tea dealers in Germany.

Design for Enthusiasts

The client's requirements for the new tea brand consisted of a brand name development with an international touch that says German tea but can also be easily pronounced by English and French tea enthusiasts. Wollenhaupt assigned Braue the complete design of all brand elements.

OPEN HERE

In order to create a unique premium brand that reflected the long tradition of Gebrueder Wollenhaupt in an underlying way, Braue created an imaginary heritage for the brand. The story: After more than 100 years, Melissa Lindbergh, daughter of an influential Hanseatic tea merchant, finds the forgotten diaries of her great-grandfather, a tea salesman from the early years of the colonial period. From his records and notes, she learns the secrets of a unique tea blend and the distinctive qualities of the best teas in the world. With the new Lindbergh tea brand, she breathes new life into the legacy of her great-grandfather as a gift of nature to the senses of tea aficionados.

The designers gave the brand a modern vintage style to support and enhance the credibility of the Lindbergh brand story. Design details like old maps and cloth textures make the design look organic and full of life—ready to reflect the adventurous life of Gustav Lindbergh.

Packaging and More

The visual components included many elements such as the brand mark, tea sachets, packaging for 15 flavors, teacup and merchandise branding, displays, price lists, labels, stickers, business-to-business and business-to-consumer concept presentation folders, postcards, direct mailings, rack brochures, a stand-alone website, audio logo, and more.

The Lindbergh packaging concept shows how to package the brand story and reflect the emotional vibes and aura of the product. It is about much more than just wrapping the product; good packaging cares about the soul of the product.

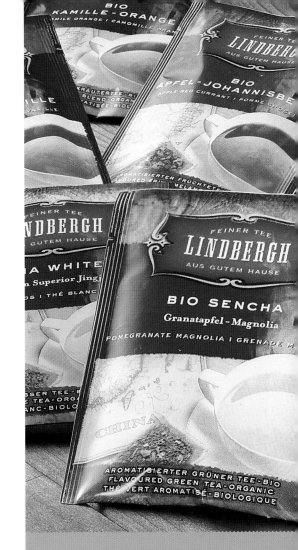

VOICE OF SUCCESS

"The idea was to project the brand's essence. Through the package design concept—which we ultimately achieved."

MARCEL ROBBERS
*Brand Design Director,
Braue-DuPuis*

Redefining a Family: A Look into **TRACTOR SUPPLY'S** Brand Unification

To achieve its aggressive growth objectives, Tractor Supply Company (TSC) sought to broaden its audience while maintaining its loyal customer base. Because most consumers in TSC trade areas own property, the company decided an upgrade of its somewhat dated and fragmented lawn and garden department would appeal to customers, both old and new. TSC turned to laga to assist with this challenge.

Laga asserted the solution required much more than an aesthetic upgrade. Rather, a solution would require a strategic umbrella brand creation, allowing for visual differentiation of multiple subcategories and designed in a manner that resonated with TSC's core customers. The new brand had to be credible to farmers and ranchers, whose use of it would validate the brand among suburbanites moving into TSC's "ruralpolitan" markets.

Reflecting Their Heritage

To achieve this, a positioning was developed that embodied TSC's sixty-plus years of lawn and garden expertise as well as its reputation for offering unique products that enable consumers to live what TSC calls the "Out Here" lifestyle. This positioning became the strategic underpinning for GroundWork, TSC's new lawn and garden brand.

Packaging Reinvention

Laga's designs encapsulate the honesty and dependability of TSC as well as the hardworking nature of its core customers. Emphasis is placed on a straightforward and clean aesthetic that doesn't overpromise on the product contents. This is achieved by use of a grid to maintain product consistency. An earth-toned color palette reflects the brand's agricultural roots. A bold font for product type throughout the lines maximizes shelf impact and ensures easy product identification.

The new private-label designs provide visual unity and improve the shopability of several lines of lawn and garden products. Dramatic growth—a sales increase of 30 percent—followed the launch of the brand in the grass seed category.

The Organic **SOURCE OF ENERGY** from the Snack Rack

The Landgarten product concept was to develop soy products that allow consumers to enjoy the entire soybean—and not in processed form, as in tofu or soy milk.

The goal was to establish Landgarten as the quality leader in the snack segment. This meant the products not only had to be healthy and taste good but also their entire packaging had to reflect this commitment to quality and taste.

From Premium Product...

The first step was to develop a premium line, sold in glass jars, that was available only in specialty food shops or wine stores. Three lines were offered: pure roasted soybeans, soybeans with spice toppings, and soybeans dipped in fine chocolate. The design featured a floral appearance with varying colors. The packaging provided a cheerful, colorful family appearance for all members of the product line.

...to Everyday Companion

A colorful and young appearance was important for the pouch packs for the grocery trade. The illustrations show situations where people enjoy eating snacks. Today, organic products no longer need to appear as traditional, farm-produced, or handmade in order to be credible. Organically grown food reflects the current trend of being more aware of food's nutritional content. This is the zeitgeist that had to be reflected by the packaging. These products called for an attractive exterior appearance that would distinguish them from the masses of drab and boring products—and d.signwerk accomplished this goal.

The soy bar concept was based on the successful recipes used for the pouch products (whole soybeans, first-class product, modern design). The designers personified the names of the products to reflect their almost human characteristics: The first members of the Landgarten Soy family are Lucy Soy and Andy Soy. D.signwerk plans to expand the family in the future.

It was important that the packaging show whole soybeans and other top-quality ingredients in addition to beautiful and appetizing product photography.

"The new design was the only way we were able to build the Landgarten brand in recent years, and also build it across Europe— although we've only just begun. And we've been able to increase our sales by almost 500 percent."

HERBERT STAVA
Founder and Managing Director,
Landgarten

"Our sales goal was to position our organic products so they would compete against conventional products at the retail grocery level. No other packaging looks as stylish and says 'premium quality' like our packaging! And retailers mention two factors behind the international listings we achieved for our products: an excellent product that has an outstanding package design!"

KERSTIN VARGA
Marketing Manager,
Landgarten

Baby's Got a **BRAND-NEW BOTTLE** in Poland, with a Perfect Sleeve to Match

It goes without saying that mothers want only the best for their babies. Bottled water with a low sodium and mineral content has appealed to consumers for years. The sales figures confirm this market trend shows no sign of losing steam. When it comes to baby nutrition, Gerber has been a household word for several generations. The trust inherent in this international brand has allowed Gerber to establish a solid base as a trendsetting leader on the Polish market with a wide range of baby foods.

Just last year, mineral water consumption in Poland rose by a robust 12 percent. Domestic competition is keen, with a large number of brands employing names including the words *mountain*, *stream*, or *spring* to equip their products with positive natural associative elements.

The Brand Comes First

Convincing mothers that Gerber water is better than other brands because it is produced especially for babies became a vital product positioning objective. The second goal was to use a visual "water" language to express the Gerber brand personality in a new packaging concept while retaining a premium look to match the worldwide branding status. Rather than relying on visuals to communicate these messages, the designers at Delikatessen started off with the bottle's shape. A series of prototypes convinced them that the bottle design must represent the essence of the brand: a soft form with no hard edges. Organic contours make the bottle easy to grip and hold safely.

OPEN HERE

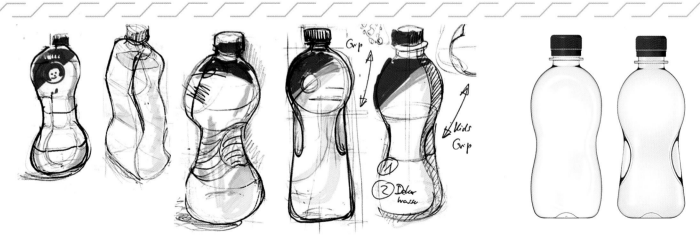

169

Shape considerations had to take different sizes into account as well. A multi-serve PET bottle in 1.4 quarts (1.18 L) and a smaller, single-serve version in 10 ounces (0.3 L) keep SKU constraints to a minimum; two nudge points provide for easier handling.

The Practical Factor

A standard cap and collar avoid unnecessary production and filling costs, but the client had reservations about the costs involved in manufacturing the thickness of the prototype's plastic. The product design was adjusted to meet the budget. A ring was added in the upper section of the bottle to give the form added stability while taking nothing away from the intended flow. In the case of the 1.4-quart (1.18 L) bottle, scaled measuring markings were added to the sides for portioning. This is a significant element of the Gerber "helping hand" concept. The water can certainly be used for drinking, yet it is equally suitable for preparing baby formula, mixing with juices and milk, or adding to teas, cereals, and meals.

Yet another practical aspect is the labeling. The PET shell suggested an ideal opportunity to use the plastic sleeve technique instead of a paper label. The sleek fit enhances the branding and product designation.

Success in the Making

Gerber is well known for coming up with solutions for the problems parents encounter in providing daily nutrition for infants, babies, and toddlers. As a market leader for jarred baby food in Poland, Gerber currently holds a 44 percent share. But this case dealt with water. The large assortment of poorly differentiated water products in Poland called for new ideas. For Delikatessen, the design objective was to create a new market segment in Poland at the top of the premium-brand range with a premium look. The positioning clearly had to portray Gerber as the only water produced especially for infants and babies due to its special mineral content.

WODA ZRODLANA

woda zródlana

WODA ZRODLANA

Woda Zródlana

woda zrodlana

woda zrodlana

WO zrodlar

Martell Teams Up with **DRAGON ROUGE** to Reassert Its Luxury Status

Martell redefined its entire brand strategy to assert the luxury status justified by the quality of its products. Following the relaunch of Martell's major classics—VS, VSOP, and Cordon Bleu, the brand's veritable jewel in Asia—designers Dragon Rouge and Martell focused their attention on the creation of a flagship reference in the world of cognac with XO. The goal was for XO to become the standard-bearer in Asia and Russia by embodying the fundamental values that characterize the brand—independent spirit, creative know-how, and enjoyment.

Rich and Multifaceted

Through the creation of a decanter and single boxed set, Dragon Rouge developed the design concept for XO that is a link between tradition and the contemporary world, between the product's French roots and its universal appeal. The bottle is graced with the highly refined lines of an arch, but the glasswork, entirely sculpted with a volute of ribbons, brings a touch of sophistication and *savoir faire*. The solid stopper, made of engraved metal, epitomizes the whole. The accompanying box expresses all the subtlety and nobility of the product

reworked in a modern way through the use of a platinum color, itself engraved with the Martell initial. With the creation of this new XO, Martell has given itself a flagship product conveying its status as a prestige brand of timeless value.

VOICE OF SUCCESS

"During the first six months after its launch (July–December, 2005), the new XO saw its sales leap by 53 percent."

2007 ANNUAL REPORT
Pernod Ricard Marketing Group

OPEN HERE

MARTELL

Creating an Elegant Design Solution for a **NEW POSITIONING**

Established in 1919, Pretty Polly is the number-one legwear brand in the United Kingdom and one of the most recognized brands for women. Because fewer women are wearing tights and stockings in the current fashion climate, Pretty Polly needed to innovate and respond to this change by developing a range of cosmetic leg products. No one owns legs quite like Pretty Polly, so this range extension was an intuitive step.

The strategy was to move the brand away from simply hosiery and to position Pretty Polly as the leg-care expert, selling gorgeous legs—legs that look great and make women feel great.

Gorgeous Legs

Brandhouse's design idea was inspired by Busby Berkeley's 1930s choreography featuring scores of chorus girls. The design echoes the strong geometric, floral, and graphic forms that celebrate and exaggerate legs. The range consists of pampering products for the day and glamour products for the evening, with a color palette to reflect the occasion and a style that has contemporary elegance.

The new range, Love Legs, was launched exclusively in Boots in September 2007 with a selection of preparatory and cosmetic leg-care products including Moisturizing Leg Shimmer, Bronzed Leg Gloss, Natural Tan Leg Bronzer, and Sheer Silk Leg Make-Up.

VOICE OF SUCCESS

"Brandhouse created a new category within leg care that is in tune with contemporary women's lifestyles in a crowded and competitive cosmetic retail enviroment."

DAVE BEARD
Creative Director,
Brandhouse

"Early feedback suggests the design has had great impact both in-store and across the pages of the beauty press."

SUE CLAGUE
Marketing Director,
Pretty Polly

OPEN HERE

The range is targeted at women who are interested in looking good, want perfect legs fast, and are influenced by fashion and celebrity trends.

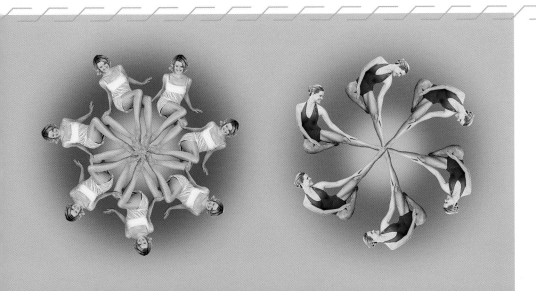

Packaging Design That **EXPLAINS AND DELIVERS** a New Usage Experience

As Procter & Gamble discovers innovative product solutions for their consumers' unmet cosmetic needs, their structural packaging needs become more challenging. The new, long-lasting formula for Cover Girl Outlast All-Day Liquid Makeup requires the consumer to apply a base of sunscreen primer followed by a finisher of All-Day Color.

Consumer satisfaction with the product depended on correct application of both products separately and in proper proportion, without substitution of a different color foundation over the primer or application of the all-day color without the sunscreen primer.

Easy to Use

Webb Scarlett deVlam (WSdV) explored a variety of two-bottle kits and side-by-side pumps in developing the Outlast foundation package. The dual design rose to the top by delivering an intuitive usage experience for the consumer.

The translucent dual bottle allows the consumer to pick her correct shade at point of sale. It also visually explains the two-step process. The single dual-orifice flip cap makes it simple to open, dispense, and apply one product at a time. Women need not search through a handbag to find a second pack, nor will a pump squirt accidentally in the handbag.

Designing Savings

The final pack, designed and engineered with two identical joined bottles, made for the lowest possible costs in mold-making and filling line adaptations. The single flip cap is the final piece in the value equation, providing significant cost savings over two caps or two pumps.

Leveraging Brand Efficacy Through
STRUCTURAL DESIGN

Prior to 2005, the mouth rinse category had long been dominated by the Listerine brand. Listerine had built an enviable 53 percent market share by consistently heralding germ-killing credentials. Although Listerine was the brand of choice in mouth rinse, the rest of the oral care aisle was overshadowed by Procter & Gamble's Crest brand.

Crest had fostered explosive growth in toothpaste and tooth-whitening products by shifting marketing from a prevention message to one of enhancement. How could Procter & Gamble leverage the compelling Crest equities to capture a bigger slice of the mouth rinse category?

A key Listerine vulnerability was an unpleasant sensory experience due to high-alcohol content. Although users believed the burning sensation proved the product worked, they generally hated the experience. Crest developed a new mouth rinse technology that offered powerful efficacy in a non-alcohol format.

Freshly Iconic

Webb Scarlett deVlam (WSdV) was commissioned to bring the new product to life on shelf and began by getting to know the consumer. WSdV did first-hand research with target consumers to see how they use and buy the product. These visits provided valuable fuel for the creative process. Crest needed a contemporary presence that could convey the product innovation and contrast with the Listerine barbell shape. An iconic form would be vital to serve as a memorable shape foundation for the brand. Logistically the shape had to be flexible to work in a range of sizes and run on existing filling lines. Judging from the success of the new product, the design clearly achieves the project objectives.

OPEN HERE

Innovation You Can See

The powerful arrowhead shape is recognizable across the store and confidently portrays product efficacy. In less than a year, Crest Pro-Health Rinse captured 10 percent of the entire mouth rinse category, including a significant portion of Listerine converts.

The launch of the Pro-Health Rinse continues to shift Crest's marketing from a message of prevention to one of enhancement.

NEW

PROVIDES DENTIST
RECOMMENDED BENEFITS

Crest®
PRO·HEALTH™
RINSE

CPC ANTIGINGIVITIS/ANTIPLAQUE ORAL RINSE

ALCOHOL FREE

KILLS GERMS THAT CAUSE:
- BAD BREATH
- PLAQUE
- GINGIVITIS

REFRESHING CLEAN MINT

1L (33.8 FL OZ)

Building Brand Value–**DRIVEN** Categories

In the early 1980s, Jamie Parham and her daughters started J&M Foods making cheese straws, a popular snack in the southern United States, based on a 100-year-old family recipe and fourth-generation tradition. The mother-daughters team stayed true to the techniques and used only the finest-quality ingredients to make this exceptionally tasty snack.

This small family business has grown into a national provider for the high-end specialty snack/gifting arena. However, twenty-five years later, J&M Foods lies at a crossroads. The company faces increasingly heated competition and continually combats the commoditization of the industry via private labels. J&M Foods can define a standout, must-have brand image, or it can drive down costs and focus on supplying private labels.

The Personal Touch

To appeal to the elitist entertainer/giver, a college-educated and often affluent 45 to 65-year-old woman, the Bright creative team felt the formal name 'J&M Foods' was too corporate for this personal gift. Through anecdotal research, they discovered consumers wanted to give homemade delicacies but didn't have the time or the skill set. By branding the package Janis & Melanie, Bright personalized the brand to build trust and connectivity.

VOICE OF SUCCESS

"Since the redesign, sales on all J&M Foods products has dramatically increased. We've had to build a new manufacturing facility to accommodate our growth."

SCOTT THIBAULT
Chief Operating Officer,
J&M Foods

"After the successful launch of the cheese straw and cookies line, the design was adapted for the tea cookies line."

KEITH BRIGHT
President and Creative Director,
Bright Strategic Design

Asiago Cheese Straws
NET WEIGHT 7 OZ (198G)

Swiss Cheese Straws
NET WEIGHT 7 OZ (198G)

Jalapeño Cheese Straws
NET WEIGHT 7 OZ (198G)

Original Cheese Straws
NET WEIGHT 7 OZ (198G)

Cookies

Chocolate Orange

Key Lime

Lemon

Chocolate Orange
Cookies
NET WEIGHT 10 OZ (283G)

Miriello Grafico Provides a **FRESH LOOK** for the Mondo Mint

With the popularity of iPod-related products, Mondo Systems recognized an opportunity to stand out in an increasingly competitive market by offering a product with ultimate usage versatility and high audio performance. Mondo teamed up with Miriello Grafico (MG) to launch their new Mondo Mint Digital Music Station, which raised the bar by offering iPod compatibility along with digital fidelity audio solutions for all music sources, including computers, MP3 players, portable CD players, gaming/audio devices, and satellite radio.

Getting Noticed

Bringing this innovative system to market meant developing a launch strategy with accompanying marketing collateral that would connect quickly with potential distributors and consumers. Critical to securing necessary sales partnerships, the packaging served as the pacesetter for establishing the product's brand look and feel. By communicating to Mondo Mint's usage scenarios while projecting a high-quality image worthy of a premium price point, the design helped open doors to discussions with key sales outlet decision makers.

Brand Expression

MG conceived the product name Mint with a corresponding identity and the tagline "Fresh Digital Fidelity," capturing the product's exceptional audio capabilities. By conducting a grassroots marketing study, customer insight provided key messaging points and visual cues targeting an unusually wide range of music lovers ages 18 to 54.

A rich palette of mint-green hues creates a flexible system of visual branding elements. The packaging design plays off the product's modern industrial attributes by utilizing open and generous spatial relationships between copy and imagery, avoiding clutter. Information is easy to grasp, and a series of icons displays product connectivity. Combined with stock imagery, custom lifestyle photography was shot to breathe life and believability into the product's functionality. Callouts throughout the packaging guide educate the viewer about the system's unique features and benefits.

VOICE OF SUCCESS

"The packaging design has played a critical role in securing ten key distribution partnerships to date, which is vital to the Mondo Mint's continued sales success."

RON GILLIES
Vice President of Sales and Marketing,
Mondo Systems, Inc.

"We look forward to leveraging the design elements of the original Mondo Mint packaging into a very cool line of Mint-inspired products."

RON MIRIELLO
President,
Miriello Grafico

Reception of the packaging design has been positive from current and potential distributors, resulting in ten partnerships to date. The product is retailed via online distributors such as Amazon.com, Buy.com, B&H Photo, Tristate, The Nerds, Beach Audio, and Mondo-usa.com. In-store retailers include RCS Experience NYC, DataVision NYC, and Best Buy test stores.

Cosmetic Brand Revival with a
STRIKING DESIGN

Bonacure is the first hair care line with a relevant variety of products to deliver hair therapy treatment for long-lasting, beautiful hair. The old design—graphic and structural—was clearly outdated and no longer accepted by the main target groups: professional hairdressers and high-end users.

A relaunch was planned to give the brand a new identity via a brand logo, a new packaging family (three-dimensional and structural), and a new design outfit. Solutions, a multidisciplinary branding and design agency in Hamburg, Germany, was given this challenging task.

Holistic Approach

The agency set out to give the Bonacure brand a new, modern, holistic approach in all dimensions:

- For the hairdressers, desirability of the product is paramount, as hairdressers distinguish themselves with the brand.
- Functionality involves finding the right product for daily practice.
- Loyalty means hairdressers must recommend their favorite hair care range with pride.
- For the personal touch, the product has to look and feel good in daily use, as target group consumers normally show off the products they use.

The reworked logo supports brand heritage while appearing modern, with simple, distinctive typography. A modern premium typeface with a therapeutically cosmetic touch was applied.

Clear and imaginative product and line names were chosen to assist and speed orientation and selection. A subtle but efficient color differentiation is pleasing to the eye, and a playful depiction of matte, glossy, and soft-touch elements round out the harmonious combination of form and graphics.

"The successful symbiosis of aesthetics and positioning appeals to all target groups: the in-shop consumer, the hairdresser, and our client!"

BETTINA GABRIEL
*Board Member & Founder,
Solutions*

It Takes More Than a
GREAT PRODUCT

The pet supply (non-food) business is crowded with mid-level brands and small specialty companies. What it lacked was a top-quality, strongly branded, and aggressively marketed line targeting upscale pet owners and retailers. This opportunity led T&K Pet Products to the doors of Sandstrom Design.

Working with independent copywriter Leslee Dillon, Sandstrom Design developed the new company name, Castor & Pollux Pet Works, as well as the entire brand personality, packaging, and store presentation. The name is based on the Gemini twins but refers to the cat and dog that "founded" the company in order to create products pets truly like.

This concept led to brand slogans like "Paw Made," "We make stuff we like," and "No humans were harmed in the production of this product." It also led to innovative product names like "Gotta Go Kitty Litter," "W.A.L.K. Dog Leash," "Wet Nose Rawhide," and "Good Buddy Cookies."

Sandstrom Design also designed stationery, marketing materials, in-store displays, and a trade show booth for Castor & Pollux Pet Works.

"The market responded positively. Sales have been brisk since introduction, and the line is now sold in high-end grocery chains and specialty stores as well as home furnishings retailer Restoration Hardware."

JON OLSEN
Creative Director,
Sandstrom Design

"The packaging has a playful yet sophisticated sensibility that speaks directly to me as an animal lover."

FOCUS GROUP CONSUMER

A Tribute to **ORIGINALITY**

Nearly bankrupt, but carrying a storied sports legacy and counter-culture cool factor, Converse came to Sandstrom Design for the development of an integrated new branding program. The Sandstrom team studied its history, distant and recent, and recommended it be strategically and graphically combined. This would allow Converse to build on its unique strengths (heritage, basketball domination, contrarian brand, Chuck Taylor All-Stars) and distinctly differentiate from more dominant competitors.

First to emerge was a new identity toolkit, which was quickly applied to business papers, product boxes/packaging, and environmental systems. Sandstrom recommended that several elements of the ubiquitous and long-lasting All-Star shoes become part of the branding, including the rubber patterned sole, white with red line base, and grommeted air vents. These elements now appear on most of Converse's product boxes, hang-tags, point-of-sale fixtures, and collateral.

Building Awareness

The designers also created a complete store-in-store system for Converse, attempting to win the competitive battle for mind share and market share in the retail battlefield. Strong graphics and flexible display systems were created to build immediate awareness in the right way: Converse and basketball are perma-nently and forever linked. The company can't outspend the competition, but it can focus on its unique strengths and respond to strong market trends that are turning away from painfully hip and punishingly omnipresent brands like Nike.

Sandstrom Design has provided product design, showroom design, retail space planning and design, sales presentations, sub-brand naming/iconography, catalog design and production, and worked extensively on several strategic initiatives. Two years after Sandstrom started the redesign, Converse was in the black and purchased by Nike.

"The Chuck Taylor brand transcends generational cultural and socio-economic boundaries. It has evolved beyond performance into an American and global youth symbol of originality and individuality."

2007 CONVERSE PRESS RELEASE

"Converse has grown to become a billion-dollar comp-any and one of the jewels of Nike's sub-brand strategy."

JACK PETERSON
President,
Sandstrom Design

Redesign Sets a **NEW STANDARD** for a Mainstream Category

Reinvent, refine, and reintroduce. Optima has done more than redesign Miller; it has repositioned it for greater sales and increased growth in an ever-changing marketplace. For Miller Genuine Draft, targeting a more sophisticated and discerning consumer, it was critical to capture the essence of a beer that should be savored and celebrated. Optima spearheaded an aggressive identity campaign that repositioned Miller Genuine Draft with all-new brand graphics, packaging, point-of-sale, fleet, and collateral materials.

Milller Genuine Draft was introduced in 1986 as the original cold-filtered packaged draft beer. Miller uses an exclusive process that prevents the beer's flavor from being heated away.

In the early 1990s, Miller Genuine Draft became Miller's main export brand, but as consumer tastes shifted to lighter mainstream beers, the brand suffered a decline in sales, as did the entire domestic full-calorie beer segment.

VOICE OF SUCCESS

"SABMiller is the world's second largest brewer, with major operations in over sixty countries and Miller Genuine Draft is one of Miller's largest brands.

There comes a time when you're ready to move on to something better."

TERRY HALEY
*MGD Brand Manager,
Miller Brewing Co.*

"The enhanced look highlights the quality of the beer inside the packaging...while better catching the eye of consumers at retail."

ERV FREDERICK
*Product Manager,
Miller Brewing Co.*

OPEN HERE

Miller®
GENUINE
Draft
COLD-FILTERED™
LAGER BEER
12 FL.OZ. 355ML
MILLER BREWING CO., MILWAUKEE, WI U.S.A.-BEER

The Attitude

Absorbing the true intrinsic nature of beer, the focus on the product became overwhelmingly important. Because the consumer related so closely to the golden yellow color, there emerged an opportunity to use beer as a backdrop and an icon for the brand. The signage and secondary packaging now maintains this bright, uplifting, and golden backdrop for the black band that houses the Miller Genuine Draft brand. The circular pour brings your eye into the branding and invites you to be part of the experience.

The sophistication of the typography gives Miller Genuine Draft its quality and authenticity. Centering the brand on the packaging also gives the band a sense of pride and authority.

Intelligence at Hand

Looking at the primary graphics and structure, Optima chose to keep the clear glass bottle in order to show off the beauty and appetite appeal of the product. The applied plastic label also allows the consumer to view the product directly through the branding. This labeling process also helps elevate the quality perception of the beer and branding.

The creation of the Miller Genuine Draft seal that appears on the label also gives the branding an award winning message. Association of the seal with the Frederick Miller signature brings us back to the purity and authenticity of the product.

The graphic language of the packaging graphics are also a reflection of other key products that are associated with consumers. Borrowing from the attitude is offered by cigar and spirit packaging, the Miller Genuine Draft's visual language aspires to feel both unique and award winning.

Maintaining a strong system architecture and brand guidelines, the overall brand experience continues to deliver on the key product attribute of superior taste.

Targeting a more sophisticated consumer and capturing the true essence of beer that should be savored and celebrated, Optima has truly reinvented the Miller Genuine Draft brand.

Miller
GENUINE
Draft

COLD - FILTERED™

CRAFTING A Premium Position

AGLH, an Argentine producer of honey, was in need of a new brand identity and a distinctive packaging design for its premium range of honeys, Estancia Las Quinas. The main goal was to succeed overseas in some of the most demanding markets in Europe and North America. To meet the objective, the brand identity had to radiate premium export quality and great purity.

The strategy planning by Tridimage, the design consultancy entrusted with this project, included a strong graphic communication of a key distinctive value of the product: the uniqueness of its place of origin.

The graphic concept relies on the particularities of the Argentine pampas—its vast extension, the poetry of its landscape, and its natural purity. To magnify the product's impact, the communication leverages the fantasies of the foreign consumer, positioning the brand from a poetic angle. Translating poetry into images, design was aimed at seducing both local and global consumers. Since the Estancia Las Quinas range of products includes a wide diversity of honey, each flavor type was identified by a distinctive color and a different photograph featuring an extreme close-up of local flora.

The chosen script font contributes a warm soul for the logo, reminiscent of the company's first steps and its commitment to quality. The subtle graphic balance between purity and warmth is, in fact, a reflection of the rare communion of two foundational values of Estancia Las Quinas honeys: up-to-date machinery combined with the most natural source. The consequent packaging design is as striking as it is distinguishing, perfectly fitting the product's uniqueness.

In less than a year, Estancia Las Quinas honeys have managed to buzz all around the globe, becoming a strong competitor in markets including the United States, Germany, and Japan—and an instant hit in Argentina, their homeland.

Developing INTERNATIONAL APPEAL

Sabores y Placeres is a new Argentine super-premium smoked food producer specializing in a wide variety of Patagonian fish and meats, including salmon, trout, pork, turkey, duck, deer, and wild boar, commercialized under its main brand, Ahumalén.

The challenge was to convey Ahumalén's primary equities as an exquisite, traditionally crafted, smoked delicatessen from Argentina through a new brand image and product packaging that would allow it to find a place in the upper range of the premium international market.

As the category was flooded with homemade-looking products, Tridimage decided to try a more refined approach in order to stand out. Black, gold foil, metallic ink, and a different color coding for each variety compose the spine of the package design, which aims for an elegant, subtle, yet tempting quality. A window exposes the content so consumers can see the fresh product within.

On the technical side, the packs are offset printed on 350-gram cardboard, with gloss spot UV varnish finishing and matte gold foil details. Two transparent stickers on both front and back make for a clearer communication of each variety and provide mandatory information and nutrition facts. The results of the redesign were immediate. Ahumalén is currently making strong inroads in both local and foreign markets.

VOICE OF SUCCESS

"At retail, consumers rapidly identified the brand as the category leader. Our products have been [welcomed] thanks to our packaging design, which has been a major key to success for this line of products."

GUSTAVO AZULAY
Executive Chef,
Sabores y Placeres

"The brand's logo and name, the background image, and the shape of the die-cut window refer to the sensual smoke inherent of the production process that characterizes these gourmandises, allowing an instant recognition of the value vector of the brand at the point of purchase."

HERNÁN BRABERMAN
Design Director and Partner,
Tridimage

AHUMALÉN®
Manjares Artesanales

Salazón de Pato
Al estilo
AHUMADO

AHUMALÉN®
Manjares Artesanales

Kassler
Lomo de
Cerdo cocido
Abumado con Ciruelo

CURADO Y ADITIVADO
CONTENIDO NETO 100g

INDUSTRIA A

AHUMALÉN®
Manjares Artesanales

Salmón
Ahumado
con Nogal
AHUMADO EN FRIO

CONTENIDO NETO 100g

197

JAFFA—The Most Renowned Israeli Brand in the World

Jaffa is an ancient port city located on the Mediterranean Sea, just south of Tel Aviv. It's a perfect climate for agriculture, especially for growing bananas and citrus fruits. In fact, easy-to-peel Jaffa or Shamouti seedless oranges are world-famous for their sweetness.

Jaffa Gold is a trade name for a line of premium 100 percent natural drinks, juices, and nectars made from a variety of different fruits. The factory that manufactures Jaffa Gold belongs to Kibbutz Gan-Shmuel Foods, one of Israel's largest food exporters. Due to the socialist structure of the Kibbutz community, all members have joint ownership of all the assets, including the Jaffa Gold brand. This is an extremely significant and sensitive point that needed to be considered in all stages of the decision-making process with respect to the brand and the business.

Fresh Direction

The previous packaging for Jaffa Gold was tired and outdated, which contributed to declining sales and low product distribution. A redesign that would suggest freshness and quality was necessary, but at the same time, the products needed to be familiar and recognized by consumers.

Studio Eldad Shaw focused on creating a design that would capture the essence of Jaffa Gold's mouth-watering fruits. In keeping with the goal of portraying freshness and high quality, the designers realized that simple graphics would best achieve this. By not cluttering the design, Studio Eldad Shaw wanted the customer to stay focused on the natural taste of the beverage, and immediately want to enjoy it.

Universal Appeal

The new design was approved by all of the brands' decision makers, and the packaging's bold simplicity thrilled existing consumers and attracted new ones.

SAN BENEDETTO Flavored Water
Creating Taste Without its Display

San Benedetto is an elite, low-mineral delicacy. This Italian brand of water was arguably the original favorite of the Republic of Venice, in vogue with aristocratic Venetian families during the Renaissance. The water, tapped at the surface in ancient times, is now drawn from San Benedetto Springs, 1,000 feet (305 m) below ground to ensure that all its original features are unchanged, and unadulterated. The water trickles down from an Alpine glacier peak to be bottled, untouched by human hands, and sold throughout the world.

Something New

Tempo Beverages, Ltd., hired Studio Eldad Shaw to design the packaging for San Benedetto's new flavored mineral waters. Although mineral water has been in the Israeli market for several years, San Benedetto is the first flavored mineral water to be marketed there.

Because the product is colorless, yet tastes of fresh fruit, Studio Eldad Shaw needed to create a package design that conveyed the flavor distinctions. They also had to adhere to strict constraints imposed by the Israeli Health Depart-

ment, which forbids the use of fruit illustrations on products containing less then 45 percent fruit. The design conveys freshness and a natural full-flavored taste. Since launch, San Benedetto Flavored Water has become known as a premium soft drink and found its way to consumers mouths and hearts.

OPEN HERE

"San Benedetto Flavored Water became known as a premium soft drink and found its way to our consumers' mouths and hearts."

YOASH BEN-ELIEZER
Director of Marketing,
Tempo Beverages Ltd.

Tea Packaging So Bold and Opinionated, It's **FULLY LOADED**

Tired of mass-produced, dust-filled tea bags, sour herbal teas, and tasteless green and black teas, Fully Loaded Tea set out to change the category with unique flavors and special tea bags. By defying category norms with its tagline, "Fully Loaded Tea, for a watered-down world," Subplot Design created a brand that marries a strong brand story with a strong product that consumers and retailers have found compelling.

The Design System

Building on an opinionated and humorous take on the "watered-down world," flavor names jump out of bold, personality-driven stories that are printed on every package. Flavor-inspired painted backgrounds, illustrated ingredients, and iconic photography bring the stories to life. A combination of lush, descriptive flavor profiles, brewing instructions, and the Fully Loaded Tea story balance out a brand that's here to inform as well as provoke.

OPEN HERE

Above: A frosted Plexiglas counter-top display allows the product, not the display, to be the hero. A unique drop-down drawer avoids the typical messy perforated opening.

Let's Face It:
The **ROCAMOJO** Brand Rocks!

Rocamojo is a roasted soy-based coffee alternative for the health-conscious coffee connoisseur. Its unique formula for roasting soybeans was originally created by a Southern California chiropractor in his garage to aid with his clients' desire for rich, full-bodied, and aromatic coffee drink flavor without the anxiety surge associated with caffeinated coffee. The success of Rocamojo grew quickly by word of mouth, but the original package was not on par with the level of its competitors, especially in the mass-market arena it wanted to enter.

Evenson Design Group (EDG) wanted to create a friendly package that would jump off the shelves and compete head-to-head in a highly competitive sea of coffee and soy-based alternative products. Additionally, EDG wanted to develop an equally attractive package for the half-soy, half-gourmet coffee Rocamojo Blend that would complement the original package design.

Rocamojo Man

After looking at nationwide mass-market coffee brands, as well as the soy-based alternatives carried by small, independent health food stores, EDG's strategy was to create a brand with a built-in spokesperson: the Rocamojo man. This smiling, but quirky, square-faced humanoid gave the Rocamojo package an approachable quality on store shelves and at home. The final brand identity and package design featured a primitive style illustration juxtaposed with a captivating color palette and customized typography.

Successful Results

The package design played an integral role in the nationwide success of the products' sales as well as instant publicity and exposure. The product was embraced and purchased by top-tier retailers with a national footprint, including Whole Foods, Cost Plus World Markets, Wild Oats, and Gelson's.

OPEN HERE

net wt 16 oz (453g)

ROCAMOJO™

roasted soy

a healthy coffee alternative

caffeine free

certified organic

Less **IS MORE**: Streamlined Messaging Appeals to Discerning Segment

The image of Swell Ice Tea is designed to seduce, using elements more commonly found in the perfume world than the beverage world. The designers at Ruiz & Co. started with a palette of dense tones that evokes the flavors of the products in this line. On top of these colors they added subtle illustrations of tea plants—almost shadows— keeping the design minimal and clean to appeal to a sophisticated, mainly female audience.

In order to seduce without being obvious, the name of the product and the logo are discreetly placed. In contrast, each product was assigned a number that becomes the most important graphic element, enveloping the product in an air of mystery at first glance. The typefaces are basic sans serifs to offset the baroque nature of the colors and give the design the modernity and forcefulness it requires.

Ice Tea Emerges

The herbal tea market comprises new flavors and blends. While the consumption of classic products (Earl Grey, mint, chamomile, and so on) has stagnated, the new specialties are growing at a significant rate. The consumer of hot herbal teas will be interested in an iced tea with the same connotations in a different moment of consumption.

In numerous Asian countries, tea has been recognized for its medicinal qualities for over 5,000 years. The pharmaceutical and dental sectors have focused on the characteristics of different teas supported by the latest studies, and they are developing product in this niche.

The iced tea market was founded in the United States in 1904, during the international expo in St. Louis, Missouri. Today 11 billion liters (10.4 billion quarts) of ice tea are consumed annually. The United States is the leading iced tea market, representing four-fifths of consumed tea worldwide.

Nestea is the leading product, with over 80 percent of the market share. Supported by the Coca-Cola distribution network, it is carrying out major marketing campaigns on television and in magazines. It also receives significant promotional support from point-of-purchase (POP) advertising during the summer.

Strategic Design

Swell Iced Tea inaugurated the new market trend of isotonic beverages with a low-calorie content. Supported by the strong growth of iced tea consumption in Spain, it is differentiated from other available products by seeking consumers who desire a product that provides added value. Swell's target consumers are athletic, upper-middle class 30–45-year-old females, so the marketing had to appeal to this audience.

01
ICE GREEN TEA
stimulant

Swell

02
ICE RED TEA
relax

Swell

03
ICE WHITE TEA
tonic

Swell

HERE

How to Create a Fresh, **NEW LOOK**
Using the Right Visual Language

The body wash product segment has been experiencing double-digit growth, but Dial has been growing at a much slower rate. Competition grew with the increasing introduction of new soap brands to the marketplace.

To remain competitive, Dial needed to reinvent and modernize Dial Body Wash in both message and design; consolidate Dial Daily Care and Dial Antibacterial under one common marketing message: Differentiate and stand out on the shelf as a unified family, and develop distinct communication for each product variant.

Attracting the Family

To appeal to an all-family demographic, especially the 18–49 year olds, as the primary purchasers, designers at Ciulla Associates worked to create a contemporary Dial look that highlighted a promise of "Healthier Skin, Healthier You."

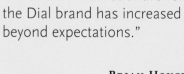

VOICE OF SUCCESS

"As a result of the very successful body wash line introduction, the design was extended to bar soaps and new liquid hand soaps."

SAM J. CIULLA
CEO and Executive Creative Director,
Ciulla Associates

"Since the redesign, sales have increased considerably and the overall market share for the Dial brand has increased beyond expectations."

BRIAN HOUCK
Director,
Creative Services,
The Dial Corporation

OPEN HERE

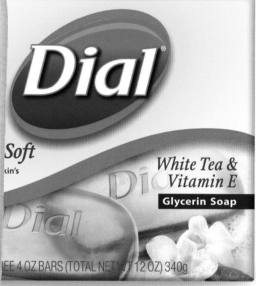

Packaging Reinvention

Ciulla designed the packages with a consistent communication hierarchy, to create shelf recognition. The Dial logo is prominent in all package variations, with the sub-group (for example, Clean and Fresh) next visible, followed by the fragrance, which is showcased through color, imagery, and descriptive copy.

The new designs consolidated the vast product line with a consistent visual language that delivers against the positioning "Healthier Skin, Healthier You."

Nature vs. Science

During phase one exploration, Ciulla Associates developed a visual language around the positioning. This language inspired the design team to create a variety of design solutions that communicated "skin wellness" along with many of the key attributes of the brand and its target audience. The designers provided a spectrum of solutions emphasizing "the reason to believe" as a technological advancement called "skin-balancing actives" and ending with a "naturally derived" healthy, clean takeaway. This range of work helped determine how important a science link was for the brand. Consumer research confirmed the naturally derived story as more compelling than a heavy clinical or cosmeceutical design approach. This allowed subsequent phases to focus on beautiful photographic imagery to convey the fragrances and the proposition "a healthy clean you can feel."

An Everyday Value Becomes
BREEZY AND BEAUTIFUL

Purex laundry detergent is the second-largest-selling brand detergent in a $4.8 billon (£2.4 billion) category, but it was suffering from mediocre to low brand perception. Purex was seen as a value player that did not possess the primary strengths of the mid- and premium-tier laundry brands. The Purex brand needed to strengthen its perceived cleaning abilities and gain a new audience while retaining current value-brand shoppers.

Uplifting the Brand Character
While the color blue was recognized as Purex's brand color, the existing packaging had no other significant brand equities client and consumers felt strongly about. The brand's perception was "dated, tired, and industrial;" consumers described the package as reminiscent of a "motor oil container." Designers at Ciulla Associates elevated and energized the graphics to express Purex's new brand position of "Pure Clean Living" and increase the perception of cleaning power. The use of motion cues reinforced strong cleaning, and fragrance imagery supported the products' freshening performance.

Impact, Clarity, Shopability
With the Purex franchise comprising over 125 SKUs in the United States and Canada, it was essential to achieve the right balance of shelf impact while clearly communicating sub-brand and fragrance differentiation for ease of shopability. Variants and fragrances are clearly identified for the shopper.

Before

The final design uses breezy, outdoor-fresh illustrations to reinforce the brand essence and to stand out on a shelf full of flat, hard-hitting graphics.

Creating a **PREMIUM LOOK** Consumers Feel Proud to Purchase

After years of strong results as a private-label supplier, the Sugar Plum Fairy Baking Company was ready to market and grow their own brand name. To launch this family-owned and operated brand of handmade, all-natural baked goods, Crave aimed to create packaging with naturally refined, premium character, maintaining relevance to consumer needs and category cues. A selection of expressive words communicates the concise visual voice Crave identified to represent the Sugar Plum brand: special, dreamy, delectable, all-natural, handmade, and gourmet. Using the visual voice as a guide, Crave designed packaging with exquisite style, detail, and on-shelf impact.

Visually Delicious

Crave's design fosters a sense of everyday indulgence for the Sugar Plum Fairy brand. Focusing on Sugar Plum's gourmet, high-quality products and eschewing clutter simplifies and amplifies the brand's voice. The result is a visually delicious retail success.

OPEN HERE

FLOURLESS
CHOCOLATE * RAS
— ALL NATURAL TO

as delicious as your dreams™

TIRAMISU
— ALL NATURAL —

Keep Frozen
Net Wt 32 oz (908g)

ON * RASPBERRY
LL NATURAL TART —

Keep Frozen
Net Wt 16 oz (454g)

Following its successful launch, Sugar Plum
expanded with a distinctive brand extension:
holiday cookie tins. Crave designed tins using
key brand elements plus original illustration
for keepsake artistry.

Meeting New Customer Demands with
a **STORYTELLING DESIGN CONCEPT**

Since the late nineteenth century, the Maggi brand has maintained its reputation for traditional cooking while continuing to appeal to new generations. As a high-quality cooking aid, the range of Maggi Fix products fills the gap between homemade and fast food, which meets the culinary desire of many people. Since their market launch, the inconspicuous little pouches have emerged as the most important line within the Maggi product range and the leading brand in the product segment. However, today Maggi finds itself in a head-to-head race with its competitors, which forced the company to reconsider the concept and positioning of the products.

Shift in Culinary Preferences

According to consumers' current desire for home-cooked meals and freshness, the strategic design concept emphasizes the enjoyment factor and moves the enormous variety of Maggi Fix products to the center of attention.

The Never-ending Cookbook

The revised design of the package is simple: The rectangular standard packaging takes the shape of a flipped-open cookbook; it stands out from the competition and makes an immediate link to easy cooking. It conveys the range of Fix products that gives culinary inspiration day after day. The design is supported by the repositioned sub-brand, Frisch, which translates to "freshness and indulgence." Additionally, all the fresh ingredients required for a complete meal are listed in cookbook style.

The food photography in the foreground raises appetite appeal and encourages customers to experience their own culinary moment. Color codes on the left faciliate the product search by symbolizing the Fix categories: meat, fish, vegetables, and pasta.

OPEN HERE

Before

After

The design follows Maggi's new positioning strategy. It emphasizes great variety with homemade quality—an emotional plus.

Creating a Successful Brand
with a **PERSONAL TOUCH**

Karen's Botanicals creates exquisite body care products using the highest-quality herbs and the purest natural ingredients available. Formed by traditional and contemporary herbal wisdom, most of the products begin with fresh and organic plants that, like whole foods, contain a wide spectrum of nourishing compounds. When Karen Palcho decided to make the leap from a hobby to a business, her goal was to have beautiful packaging to increase sales in a highly competitive marketplace.

Embodying Nature

Partners Design focused on Palcho's products, processes, and philosophy, drawing inspiration from nature and vibrant, yet aged, colors. The team used an enticing combination of colors, serif and handwritten typography, plus carefully manipulated original photography to appropriately represent each variant in the product line. Backgrounds change from product to product, but all colors work beautifully together as well as on their own to create a compelling line.

VOICE OF SUCCESS

"These labels enabled my product to stand out amidst hundreds of companies producing similar lines."

KAREN PALCHO
Principal,
Karen's Botanicals

"Our goal was to create beautiful visuals that would make it difficult for consumers to overlook this product."

CHRIS WERNER
Creative Director,
Partners Design, Inc.

OPEN HERE

Karen's Botanicals — Soothing Calendula Rose Oil for babies and mothers

K
KAREN'S BOTANICALS
K° C°
[60 ML]
2 fl. oz.

KAREN'S BOTANICALS
K

SPICING UP an Already Spicy Product

Buffalo Wild Wings Grill & Bar is one of the top ten fastest-growing U.S. restaurant chains. The consumers enter a world of entertainment that starts with big-screen sports and continues with a series of eye-catching menus packed with wing trivia, insider information, customer proclamations, and party talk. And, of course, great food.

Serious Sauce Appeal

"More than a dozen signature sauces to spice up your world." That's a key differentiator of the Buffalo Wild Wings brand, so Larsen proclaimed it by redesigning the sauce bottle labels on a color continuum that ranges from smilin' (signified by greens and yellows) to screamin' (signified by oranges and reds). As Buffalo Wild Wings develops new sauces, the continuum can easily accommodate them.

Each sauce label features a bold Buffalo circle icon and, for the first time, a concise flavor description. Previously, guests had to ask the waitstaff in order to learn whether, say, Caribbean Jerk was hotter than Mango Habanero. Larsen then created an entire menu page for these brand-defining sauces, letting consumers see the entire lineup on the menu. The result: Boost retail sauce sales and position Buffalo Wild Wings as the leader in wing sauce.

OPEN HERE

VOICE OF SUCCESS

"Food contributes to 70 percent of the revenue at Buffalo Wild Wings, so behind the fun of the menu and sauce bottle design was solid menu science—to help the client increase gross profit and optimize the average check. Since, the redesign, shares have risen 61 percent."

SALLY SMITH
*President & CEO,
Larsen*

A Clean Look with **PERSONALITY**

Leveraging the growing popularity of sake in the United States, three San Francisco Bay Area wine industry veterans created a brand new sake drink. Saké 2 Me is the first bottled drink to blend pure, premium, junmai sake (very pure rice sake) with exotic all-natural Asian flavors. It is a lightly sparkling and refreshingly clean cocktail that was launched in 2007 in four flavors: ginger mango, yuzu citrus, Asian pear, and green tea. The client wanted to tap into the popularity of wine coolers, hard lemonades, and vodka/rum/tequila cocktails with young adult consumers.

East Meets West

The San Francisco–based graphic design firm MOD/Michael Osborne Design, Inc. worked with their clients to develop Saké 2 Me's brand design. The creative team identified and captured the brand's personality—bold, Asian, contemporary, yet definitely American.

Saké 2 Me is being marketed in upscale bars and restaurants as a trendy adventurous alternative, particularly to beer. The grassroots strategy of touring popular bars and restaurants, meeting owners and managers, has given the client an edge in reaching Saké 2 Me's target of 21–39-year-old consumers. With this in mind, MOD made sure the product's single-serve 6-ounce (180 ml) bottles stood out on the shelf with high-impact, easy-to-read graphics.

A Chill Palette

Taking cues from Saké 2 Me's flavors, which are fruity and ripe, with a subtle spice aroma, MOD chose a sophisticated color palette that relates well and references each of the flavor varieties. The product is served cool, as the best sakes are, and the muted exotic colors express the chill aspect. The smart, eye-catching package design, especially in the four-pack, alerts consumers that this is a handcrafted artisanal product.

Although consumers tend to skew toward female, the package design avoids the overtly feminine, instead taking its visual cues from pared-down aspects of Japanese culture. Character icons were developed that identify a taste quality for each flavor of Saké 2 Me: Ginger mango means refreshing; yuzu means tangy citrus fruit; green tea is crisp, pure, clean, and cool; and the Asian pear is sweet and ripe. The icons are an amusing wink to consumers who speak Japanese.

Exciting Consumers

Saké 2 Me is a whole new spirits category, and response to the initial launch of this distinctive product has been enthusiastic. "The premium sake market is growing by 30 percent a year, with explosive demand during the past eighteen months," says CEO Jeff Smith, who founded the company with partners Ed Lehrman and Nick Ramkowsky. "Beer, which has always led the alcoholic beverage market, is losing share to distilled spirits and wine. And the fastest segment of the wine market is among drinkers trading upward into the premium price bracket. Our goal is to reach 100,000-case production in two years, and, if we're successful, 1 million in five years."

Cultivating a **BRAND ESSENCE** by Turning Need into Want

Gardena is the European market leader in gardening tools. The company has been in business since 1961, and the brand can be found in about 100 countries around the world. Since the 1960s, Gardena products have been perceived as the archetype of gardening tools. Their design expressed the company's brand values of the time. Developed by Swiss designer Franco Clivio, the design followed the philosophy of the Ulm school's nonemotional and democratic product design. Within a few years, the successful brand grew a catalog of over 2,000 items. Their functional form language and colorway became recogniz-able across the product range—from irrigation to power tools, including lawn care and heavy gardening tools. In 2001, Gardena decided to internationalize its brand and open itself to target groups with a younger mindset. The new design would need to create desire for the product's intended consumer.

Goals

Factor Design was asked to develop a packaging concept that could encompass all Gardena products, from sealing rings to big power lawn mowers. Since the product is distributed in 100 countries, the packaging had to communicate in up

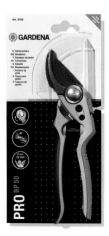

to sixteen languages. Another challenge was with the packaging itself, as it wouldn't be logistically possible to change the format of the box or blister cards.

Strategy

A clever modular system cuts the packaging face into brand area, mood, and information area. To get past the language barriers, it was necessary to replace words with photos, illustrations, and pictograms wherever possible. With a demanding briefing sheet, the project managers at Gardena were forced to limit the propositions and declarations on the product carriers to a minimum. Each unit communicates only one benefit, the so-called mega benefit.

BLACK MAGIC Lets a Design Relaunch Speak a New Visual Language

OPEN HERE

The market for pet foods has always been fiercely competitive. With so many brands on the shelves, it takes more than prime-time commercials and an easily affordable price to convince consumers that they are truly giving their pets at home the nutrition they deserve. What makes a pet-food brand "premium," and how do you communicate that?

The Fressnapf chain of stores in Germany made its name by relying on quality first, and reinforced that concept by introducing its own private-label brands. The store name refers to the typical feeding bowl used for pets. A broad spectrum of pet owners with different incomes and widely varying tastes had built up a dependable customer base.

Why Risk a Change?

The design for the private-label product line had been untouched since 2000, but the market for pet food had greatly evolved since then.

The designers at Delikatessen used color-coding, brand blocking, photos and easily understandable icons to redefine an established brand by giving it a premium aura.

Two Ways to Go

The product range offers the "classic" and "sensitive" lines. Today more information can be found on proper nutrition for pets than ever before. Not surprisingly, their digestive tracts change as they get older. Some pets react more sensitively than others. That point is now reinforced by a prominent, color-coded "sensitive" strip on the respective package front. In alignment with the key concept of premium product positioning, the designers at Delikatessen considered how the design would translate in other countries. The flavor designation, such as chicken, has been color coded in the three main languages: German, French, and English.

The brand name, age indicators, and supporting text in English, along with multilingual flavor varieties cohesively reflect global considerations. Together with strong brand blocking input, the desired premium quality has now been achieved across the board.

Every Picture Tells a Story

No matter what language or where the product is sold, the new package design contains well-balanced pictorial elements with a high appeal to pet owners. The photos are deliberately cropped, but the animals still have a contented look about them. For nutritional details, the icon bar tells a story of its own.

A Top Seller

The new package design encountered near-immediate acceptance. Concurrent with the relaunch, *Stiftung Warentest*, an unbiased German consumer product test magazine, rated the beef line for dogs "best in test," which didn't hurt sales either. The result was a sell-out, a supply shortage of the product at the Fressnapf outlets.

A client's bold resolve to make needed change and committed designers ready to take on a challenge were essential in giving "premium" pet food a new look.

OPEN HERE

SELECT GOLD®
Premium Health Formula

DIGESTION
Huhn und Reis
Poulet et Riz
Chicken and Rice

sensitive

sensitive stomach

high digestibility

intestinal flora (special fibres)

shiny skin+coat (omega 3+6)

SELECT GOLD®

HAIR + SKIN

SELECT GOLD®
Premium Health Formula

ACCEPTA

Feinste Leber

VOICE OF SUCCESS

"It's hard to say what I like
the most: the freshness, the
modern look or, to be honest,
the plain fact that it works."

JÖRG WASEL
*Marketing Director,
Fressnapf*

Chinese Consumers **TRADING UP**

The Chinese cosmetic market is growing at a rate of 15 to 20 percent, and it is anticipated to surpass the U.S. market in value by 2010. The driving force behind this surge is an active and emergent middle class that is increasingly willing to trade up for products and brands that deliver superior performance and an emotional connection.

With CleaWhite, Avon China had an existing brand that was dated, perceived as basic, and was an unrecognized and undistinguished offering in the skin-whitening segment. Whitening products are a large and growing business in China, so Avon needed a competitive entry in the segment, one that would appeal to young, middle-class women by connecting to their proactive nature—spontaneous, vital, and sophisticated.

Radiance and Vitality Through Design

CleaWhite was repositioned to provide exceptionally beautiful skin that "glows with translucency." Desgrippes Gobé first concentrated on enhancing the shape and material selection for the bottle. The vitality of the brand is characterized by the iriodine effect on the pearlized bottle material, which represents the outer light, and the radiance users feel after using CleaWhite. The rounded shape and rectangular front panel deliver a modern, sensual look that does not sacrifice the feelings of intimacy the brand needs to convey.

The new brand identity design and the outer box graphics were then designed and integrated with the new bottle to highlight the radiance and shine the brand promises. The typography is active and modern, with a sense of luxury to appeal to the active woman.

The new CleaWhite is a powerful challenger to department store counter brands in both quality and image—essential to any package in a competitive category, but especially so in the direct sales channel, where Avon lives.

OPEN HERE

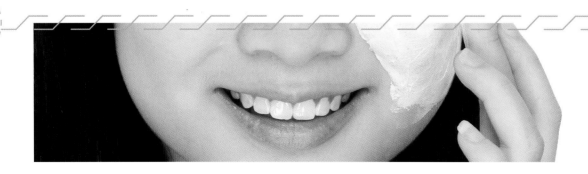

CREATING ADVENTURE
in historical ambiance

The fish delicacy store H.J. Fiedler Meeresdelikatessen GmbH is a well-established store in Bremer- haven, Northern Germany, with custom- ers from all over the country and many tourists from abroad. Founded in 1827, Bremerhaven is a seaport city with a long history as an important trade port. To cel- ebrate the 100th anniversary of the Fish- ing Hall No. 4 in 2006 (in which the shop is located), Hans Joachim Fiedler wanted to redesign and develop his shop from a rather ordinary, simple fish shop to an adventure store with many interesting and entertaining new elements.

Using all Five Senses

Fiedler wanted to bring the shopping experience in his store to the next level. After discussions and workshops with Kai Braue at Braue-DuPuis, the 'five senses' store concept was born. The new design engages visually, but also appeals with ambience incorporating tactile, audio, and olfactory aspects as well. The products themselves naturally are tasty.

VOICE OF SUCCESS

"Six months after the rebranding, our figures went up almost 20 percent in volume of sales and our company was awarded for the store of the year."

HANS-JOACHIM FIEDLER
Managing Director,
Fiedlers Fischmarkt

"If Walt Disney would have gone into the fish delicacy business, this could possibly be the store that he might have created."

MARÇEL ROBBERS
Brand Design Director,
Braue-DuPuis

Bereits als junger Mann entdeckte unser Großvater seine Liebe zu frischem Fisch und erlesenen Meeresdelikatessen. Mit Leidenschaft und dem meisterlichen Handwerk der traditionellen Fischräucherei erfüllte er sich seinen Traum vom eigenen Fischladen und legte damit den Grundstein für »Fiedlers Fischmarkt anno 1906«. Schauen Sie mal rein: www.FIEDLERS-FISCHMARKT.DE.

Bewahren Sie diese Verpackung ungeöffnet im Kühlschrank auf – somit ist eine optimale Haltbarkeit gewährleistet. Erst kurz vor Gebrauch öffnen. Zur vollen Geschmacksentfaltung dieses

Produkt ca. 30 Minuten vor Verzehr aus d... nehmen und bei Zimmertemperatur servier... Bei 2°C bis 7°C haltbar bis: siehe Etikett

FIEDLERS
FISCHMARKT
ANNO • 1906
FEINSTE MEERESDELIKATESSEN
AUS BREMERHAVEN

Bewahren Sie diese Verpackung ungeöffnet im Kühlschrank auf – somit ist eine optimale Haltbarkeit gewährleistet. Erst kurz vor Gebrauch öffnen. Zur vollen Geschmacksentfaltung dieses

Produkt ca. 30 Minuten vor Verzehr aus der Packung nehmen und bei Zimmertemperatur servieren. Bei 2°C bis 7°C haltbar bis: siehe Etikett
Informationen zur Verpackung unter www.weber-packaging.de

FIEDLERS
FISCHMARKT
ANNO • 1906
FEINSTE MEERESDELIKATESSEN
AUS BREMERHAVEN

OPEN HERE

Strategy

The Braue team redesigned the shop in a historical manner with a vintage look and feel. They segmented the 5,800-square-foot (538-square-meter) store into three themed worlds or experiences, Old Smokehouse, World of Fishing, and Historical Fishmarket—and created a guided walking tour through the store.

To boost the entertainment factor for customers many times over, Braue joined forces with a company that sets stage décors for musicals and theaters.

Sensual Components

The foundation for the historical shop was a group of fish replicas from the personal collection of the shop's owner. The whole store is staged in the year 1906 and can be discovered with all five senses. For example, in the Old Smokehouse, customers will find a vintage oven, that releases artificial steam every three minutes. In another corner are the traditional tools of a fish smoker. All fresh fish is wrapped in a reproduced historical newspaper from 1906. The cash registers are set within an old wooden lifeboat, Line Hinsch, from the 1920s.

A Real Sucess

In April 2007, the Hauptverband des Deutschen Einzelhandels (Germany's Premier Retail Association) honored Fiedlers Fischmarkt anno 1906 as Store of the Year 2007 in the food category. Furthermore, the number of customers climbed from 700,000 to more than 1 million per year.

ASGARD
196128 Saint Petersburg
Kuznetsovskiy ul, 11
Russia
7 812 369 0631
www.asgard-design.com

Boom Island Design
411 Washington Ave. N
Minneapolis, MN 55401
USA
612-343-0042
www.boomisland.com

Bloom Design
25 The Village, 101 Amies St.
London SW11 2JW
UK
020 7924 4533
www.bloom-design.com

Brand Engine
80 Liberty Ship Way, Suite 1
Sausalito, CA 94965
USA
415-339-4220
www.brandengine.com

Brandhouse
10A Frederick Close
London W2 2HD
UK
44 0 20 7262 1707
www.brandhouse.co.uk

Braue: Strategic Brand Design
Eiswerkestraße 8
27572 Bremerhaven
Germany
0471 983 82 0
www.braue.inf

Bright Strategic Design
4223 Glenooe Ave. Suite A-100
Marina Del Rey, CA 90292
USA
310-305-2565
www.brightdesign.com

CIULLA ASSOC.
325 West Huron Street
Chicago, IL 60610
USA
312-943-5995
www.ciulla-mlr.com

CBX
35 East 21st Street
New York, NY 10010
USA
212-404-7970
www.CBX.com

Consume UK
UK
www.consumeuk.com

Cornerstone Strategic Branding, Inc.
11 East 26th St, 20th Floor
New York, NY 10010
USA
212-686-6046
www.cornerstonebranding.com

Crave Design
3100 NW Boca Raton
Suite 109
Boca Raton , FL 33431
USA
561-417-0780
www.cravebrands.com

Delikatessen
Agentur für Marken und Design GmbH
Grosse Brunnenstraße 63A
22763 Hamburg
Germany
040 350 506 14
www.delikatessen-hamburg.com

Design Bridge
18 Clerkenwell Close
London ECIR OQN
UK
44 0 20 7814 9922
www.designbridge.com

Desgrippes Gobé
Unit 05-06,31/F
248 Queens Road East Wanchai
Hong Kong
China
852 3106 8722
www.dga.com

Dragon Rouge – New York
54 West 21st, Suite 905
New York, NY 10010
USA
212-367-8800
www.dragonrouge-usa.com

Dragon Rouge – Paris
32, rue Pagés BP 83
92153 Suresnes Cedex
France
33 1 46 97 50 00
www.dragonrouge.com

d.signwerk
Agentur für Werbung und Kommunikation
GmbH
Schörgenhubstraße 41_4030 Linz
Austria
43 732 313 777
www.d.signwerk.com

DuPuis Group
62 West Huron Street
Suite 1B
Chicago, IL 60610
USA
312-337-2040
www.dupuisgroup.com

Evenson Design
4445 Overland Ave.
Culver City, CA 90230
USA
310-204-1995
www.evensondesign.com

Factor Design
Schulterblatt 58
20357 Hamburg
Germany
49 40 43 25 17 99
www.factordesign.com

Feldmann + Schultchen Design Studios
Himmelstraße 10-16
22299 Hamburg
Germany
040 510000
www.fsdesign.de

Future Brand
Level 4, 520 Bourke St.
Melbourne 3000
Australia
61 3 96 04 2777
www.futurebrand.com

IMA Design
129, 21/1
5 Spasskaya
Moscow, Russia
7-465-775-4810
www.imadesign.ru

Just Blue Design
BorselstraBe 20
22765 Hamburg
Germany
49 0 40 38 60 33 0
www.justblue.de

Karim Rashid Inc.
357 West 17th. St.
New York, NY 10011
USA
212-929-8657
www.karimrashid.com

laga
990 Skokie, Blvd.
Northbrook, IL 60062
USA
847-291-0500
www.laga.com

Larsen
7101 York Avenue South
Minneapolis, MN 55435
USA
952-921-3368
www.larsen.com

Michael Nash Associates
42 – 44
Newman Street
London
W1T 1QD
44 020 7631 3370
www.michaelnashassociate.com

Michael Osborne Design (MOD)
444 De Haro Street, Suite 207
San Francisco, CA 94107
USA
415-25-0125
www.modsf.com

Miriello Grafico
1660 Logan Avenue
San Diego, CA 92113
USA
619-234-1124
www.miriellografico.com

Optima Soulsight
1899 Second Street
Highland Park, IL 60035
USA
847-681-4444
www.optimabrandvision.com

Old Navy: Gap, Inc.
555 Terry Francois Blvd
San Francisco, CA 94158
USA
451-832-1496
www.gap.com

Partners Design, Inc.
187 Koenig Road
Bernville, PA 19506
USA
610-488-7611
www.partnersdesign.net

Pearlfisher
50 Brook Green
London, W6 7BJ
UK
44 0 20 7606 8666
www.pearlfisher.com

Pentagram
1508 West Fifth Street
Austin, Texas
USA
512-476-3076
www.pentagram.com

PepsiCo Inc.
700 Anderson Hill Rd.
Purchase, NY 10577
USA
914-253-2000
www.pepsico.com

Philippe Becker Design Inc.
612 Howard St., Suite 200
San Francisco, CA 94105
USA
405-348-0054
www.pbdsf.com

Ray + Keshavan
22 Brunton Road
Bangalore 560 025
India
91 0 80 2555 0486
www.rayandkeshavan.com

RealPro
11 Spartar Street
Novoruznetsr
Russia
7-384-374-4301
www.realpro.ru

Roman & Klis
Kalkofenstrasse 51
D-71083 Herrenberg
Germany
49 7032 2002 36
www.klisdesign.com

Ruiz & Co
C/Zamora 45 5 2
Barcelona, 08022
Spain
34 932 531 780
www.ruizcompany.com

Sandstrom Design
808 SW Third Ave, Suite 610
Portland, OR 97204
USA
503-248-9466
www.sandstromdesign.com

Shapiro Walker
301 North Main St. Suite 2100
Winston-Salem, NC 27101
USA
336-725-0110
www.shapirowalker.com

Smart Design
601 W. 26th Street
18th Floor
New York, NY 10001
USA
415-255-7490
www.smartdesignworldwide.com

Solutions
Sternstrasse 117
20357 Hamburg
Germany
49 0 40 43 20 06 38
www.solutions.de

Studio 111
444 N. Wells Street Suite 301
Chicago, IL 60610
USA
312-822-0111
www.studio111.com

Studio Eldad Shaw
10 hanetzach st.
ramat hasharon
47310
Isreal
972-3-549-9997
www.eldadshaw.co.il

Subplot Design Inc,
The Mercantile Building
318 Homer St. Suite 301
Vancouver, British Columbia V6B2V2
Canada
604-685-2990
www.subplot.com

Taxi Studio
93 Princess Victoria St.
Clifton Bristol BS8 4DD
UK
44 0 117 9735151
www.taxistudio.co.uk

Thompson Design Group
725 Greenwich St.
San Francisco, CA 94133
USA
415-982-5827
www.ttdg.com

Tridimage
Av. Congreso 4607
C1431AAB
Buenos Aires
Argentina
54 11 4542 8982
www.tridimage.com

Turner Duckworth
831 Montgomery St.
San Francisco, CA 94133
USA
415-675-7777
www.turnerduckworth.com

VBAT
Pilotenstraat 41 A
1059
CH Amsterdam
Netherlands
31 0 20 750 3000
www.vbat.com

Wallace Church, Inc.
330 East 48th Street
New York, NY 10017
USA
212-755-2903
www.wallacechurch.com

Webb Scarlett deVlam
224 North Desplaines Suite 100S
Chicago, IL 60661
USA
312-575-0700
www.wsdv.com/chicago

Webb Scarlett deVlam
12 Junction Mews
London W2 1PN
UK
44 0 20 7706 8076
www.wsdv.com/london

Zunda Group
41 North Main Street
Historic South Norwalk
Connnecticut 06854
USA
203-853-9600
www.zundagroup.com

About DuPuis

DuPuis (pronounced "*dü – pwé*") is a strategic brand design agency with offices in the U.S. and Europe (Braue-DuPuis). DuPuis' expertise is their ability to translate a brand's essence into powerful visual communication. By getting to the root of consumers' emotional connections with their favorite brands, DuPuis is able to consistently contribute to the success of the clients they represent. The team has been directly responsible for the global strategic design development for a long list of brands including: ConAgra Foods, Kellogg's, Nestlé, Dreyer's, Quaker, Unilever, Dole Foods, Heinz, and Sony.

Thank You

Thank you to all of our contributors, the many talented designers and marketers who provided images and told us the stories of their work. We thank **Bobby J. Calder**, **Daniel Hachard**, **Bob Squibb**, **Terry Schwartz**, **Cheryl Swanson**, and **Rob Wallace** for their insightful interviews.

Additional thanks to some of the best packaging design firms in the world as well as their esteemed clients for their generous cooperation and participation. The authors would also like to extend special thanks to the staff of DuPuis, Braue, and the following people for their critical involvement in the completion of this book:

Marianne Büsing, *contact*
Mirco Erdmann, *design*
Raimund Fohs, *design*
Leigh Haikin, *image procurement*
Jack Halpern, *agency submissions & liaison*
Mark Henderson, *image procurement*
Susan Kinast, *product photography*
Kirian Martinez, *cybrarian & resource coordinator*
Michael Paul, *contact & administration*
Mario Soto, *production advisor*
Marina Terzich, *design*
Chris Zsarnay / Z Studios, *cover photograph*

Thank you to **Emily Potts**, **Betsy Gammons**, **David Martinell**, and **Cora Hawks** of Rockport Publishers for your support. Thanks also to **Terry Lee Stone** for her edits and contribution. Thank you to **David Goodman** for his advice and business insights over the years.

Thanks mostly to our clients. It has been a pleasure and privilege to collaborate with you over the years. You inspire us!